BONUS
COLOR CHART

Here are some colors you can use on your Web pages. The colors may look slightly different on your computer screen.

D0472611

For
on addi
Web pa
56,
a

DETACH CAREFULLY HERE

#FF3300
#CC3300 #FF6600
#993300 #FF9900 #FFCC00
#FF0000 #FFFF00
#CC0000 #CCCC00
#FF0033 #990000 #FF3333 #FFFF33 #999900 #CC9900
#CC0033 #660000 #CC3333 #CCCC33 #666600 #CC9933
#990033 #330000 #993333 #FFFF66 #999933 #333300 #996600
#660033 #663333 #FF6666 #CCCC66 #666633 #CC9966
#CC0066 #CC6666 #FFFF99 #999966 #996633
#330033 #996666 #FF9999 #CCCC99 #669900
#CC3366 #663366 #CC9999 #FFFFCC #99CC00 #663300
#660066 #FFCCCC #99CC33 #669933
#996699 #99CC66 #339900
#993399 #CC99CC #CCFFCC #66CC66 #009900
#990099 #CC66CC #FFCCFF #99CC99 #339933
#CC3399 #FF99CC #669966 #006600
#CC0099 #FF66CC #336633 #336600
#993366 #FF3399 #CCCCFF #CCFFFF #003300
#FF0099 #9999CC #99CCCC #009933
#990066 #666699 #6699CC #99FFFF #669999 #009900
#9966CC #333366 #6666CC #66CCCC #336666 #006633
#663399 #000033 #333399 #006699 #99CCFF #339999 #003333 #009966
#660099 #000066 #003366 #33CCCC #006666 #339966
#330066 #000099 #336699 #009999 #66CC99
#330099 #66CCFF #00CCCC
#003399 #0099CC
#3366CC #6699FF #3399CC
#0066CC #0099FF
#3399FF

White Silver   Gray Black

Red Maroon Purple Fuchsia Lime Yellow Olive Green Blue Navy Teal Aqua

© 1999, maranGraphics Inc.

ISBN 0-7645-6067-0

HTML TAGS

DETACH CAREFULLY HERE

© 1999, maranGraphics Inc.   Creating Web Pages with HTML Simplified®, 2nd Edition   ISBN 0-7645-6067-0

Full Color on Every Page!

Creating Web Pages with HTML
Simplified® 2nd Edition

IDG's 3-D Visual™ Series

IDG BOOKS

From **maranGraphics™**

IDG Books Worldwide, Inc.
An International Data Group Company
Foster City, CA • Indianapolis • Chicago • New York

Creating Web Pages with HTML Simplified® 2nd Ed.

Published by
IDG Books Worldwide, Inc.
An International Data Group Company
919 E. Hillsdale Blvd., Suite 400
Foster City, CA 94404
(650) 655-3000

Copyright© 1999 by maranGraphics Inc.
5755 Coopers Avenue
Mississauga, Ontario, Canada
L4Z 1R9

All rights reserved. No part of this book, including interior design, cover design, and icons, may be reproduced or transmitted in any form, by any means (electronic, photocopying, recording, or otherwise) without prior written permission from maranGraphics.

Library of Congress Catalog Card No.: 99-65421

ISBN: 0-7645-6067-0

Printed in the United States of America

10 9 8 7 6 5 4 3 2 1

Distributed in the United States by IDG Books Worldwide, Inc.
Distributed by CDG Books Canada Inc. for Canada; by Transworld
Publishers Limited in the United Kingdom; by IDG Norge Books for Norway; by
IDG Sweden Books for Sweden; by IDG Books Australia Publishing Corporation
Pty. Ltd. for Australia and New Zealand; by TransQuest Publishers Pte Ltd. for
Singapore, Malaysia, Thailand, Indonesia, and Hong Kong; by Gotop Information
Inc. for Taiwan; by ICG Muse, Inc. for Japan; by Norma Comunicaciones S.A. for
Colombia; by Intersoft for South Africa; by Eyrolles for France; by International
Thomson Publishing for Germany, Austria and Switzerland; by Distribuidora
Cuspide for Argentina; by LR International for Brazil; by Galileo Libros for
Chile; by Ediciones ZETA S.C.R. Ltda. for Peru; by WS Computer Publishing
Corporation, Inc. for the Philippines; by Contemporanea de Ediciones for
Venezuela; by Express Computer Distributors for the Caribbean and West Indies;
by Micronesia Media Distributor, Inc. for Micronesia; by Grupo Editorial Norma
S.A. for Guatemala; by Chips Computadoras S.A. de C.V. for Mexico; by Editorial
Norma de Panama S.A. for Panama; by American Bookshops for Finland.
Authorized Sales Agent: Anthony Rudkin Associates for the Middle East
and North Africa.
For corporate orders, please call maranGraphics at 800-469-6616.
For general information on IDG Books Worldwide's books in the U.S.,
please call our Consumer Customer Service department at 800-762-2974.
For reseller information, including discounts and premium sales, please
call our Reseller Customer Service department at 800-434-3422.
For information on where to purchase IDG Books Worldwide's books
outside the U.S., please contact our International Sales department at
317-596-5530 or fax 317-596-5692.
For consumer information on foreign language translations, please contact
our Customer Service department at 1-800-434-3422, fax 317-596-5692,
or e-mail rights@idgbooks.com.
For information on licensing foreign or domestic rights, please phone
1-650-655-3109.
For sales inquiries and special prices for bulk quantities, please contact
our Sales department at 650-655-3200.
For information on using IDG Books Worldwide's books in the classroom
or for ordering examination copies, please contact our Educational Sales
department at 800-434-2086 or fax 317-596-5499.
For press review copies, author interviews, or other publicity information, please
contact our Public Relations department at 650-655-3000 or fax 650-655-3299.
For authorization to photocopy items for corporate, personal, or educational use,
please contact maranGraphics at 800-469-6616.

LIMIT OF LIABILITY/DISCLAIMER OF WARRANTY: THE PUBLISHER AND AUTHOR HAVE USED THEIR BEST EFFORTS IN PREPARING THIS BOOK. THE PUBLISHER AND AUTHOR MAKE NO REPRESENTATIONS OR WARRANTIES WITH RESPECT TO THE ACCURACY OR COMPLETENESS OF THE CONTENTS OF THIS BOOK AND SPECIFICALLY DISCLAIM ANY IMPLIED WARRANTIES OF MERCHANTABILITY OR FITNESS FOR A PARTICULAR PURPOSE. THERE ARE NO WARRANTIES WHICH EXTEND BEYOND THE DESCRIPTIONS CONTAINED IN THIS PARAGRAPH. NO WARRANTY MAY BE CREATED OR EXTENDED BY SALES REPRESENTATIVES OR WRITTEN SALES MATERIALS. THE ACCURACY AND COMPLETENESS OF THE INFORMATION PROVIDED HEREIN AND THE OPINIONS STATED HEREIN ARE NOT GUARANTEED OR WARRANTED TO PRODUCE ANY PARTICULAR RESULTS, AND THE ADVICE AND STRATEGIES CONTAINED HEREIN MAY NOT BE SUITABLE FOR EVERY INDIVIDUAL. NEITHER THE PUBLISHER, NOR AUTHOR SHALL BE LIABLE FOR ANY LOSS OF PROFIT OR ANY OTHER COMMERCIAL DAMAGES, INCLUDING BUT NOT LIMITED TO SPECIAL, INCIDENTAL, CONSEQUENTIAL, OR OTHER DAMAGES. FULFILLMENT OF EACH COUPON OFFER IS THE RESPONSIBILITY OF THE OFFEROR.

Trademark Acknowledgments

maranGraphics Inc. has attempted to include trademark information for products, services and companies referred to in this guide. Although maranGraphics Inc. has made reasonable efforts in gathering this information, it cannot guarantee its accuracy.

All brand names and product names used in this book are trade names, service marks, trademarks, or registered trademarks of their respective owners. IDG Books Worldwide and maranGraphics Inc. are not associated with any product or vendor mentioned in this book.

FOR PURPOSES OF ILLUSTRATING THE CONCEPTS AND TECHNIQUES DESCRIBED IN THIS BOOK, THE AUTHOR HAS CREATED VARIOUS NAMES, COMPANY NAMES, MAILING ADDRESSES, E-MAIL ADDRESSES AND PHONE NUMBERS, ALL OF WHICH ARE FICTITIOUS. ANY RESEMBLANCE OF THESE FICTITIOUS NAMES, COMPANY NAMES, MAILING ADDRESSES, E-MAIL ADDRESSES AND PHONE NUMBERS TO ANY ACTUAL PERSON, COMPANY AND/OR ORGANIZATION IS UNINTENTIONAL AND PURELY COINCIDENTAL.

maranGraphics has used their best efforts in preparing this book. As Web sites are constantly changing, some of the Web site addresses in this book may have moved or no longer exist. maranGraphics does not accept responsibility nor liability for losses or damages resulting from the information contained in this book. maranGraphics also does not support the views expressed in the Web sites contained in this book.

Permissions

Allaire HomeSite
Copyright © Allaire Corporation 1995-1999. All rights reserved.
Used by permission.

Apple Computer
Macintosh is a trademark of Apple Computers Inc., registered in the United States and other countries. Screen shots reprinted with permission from Apple Computers, Inc.

Jasc Software
Paint Shop Pro is a Trademark of Jasc Software, Inc.

Microsoft Corporation
Screen shots reprinted with permission from Microsoft Corporation.

Netscape
Copyright 1999 Netscape Communications Corporation. All rights reserved.

Permissions Granted
Flower Stop
Sunkist

©1999
maranGraphics, Inc.

The 3-D illustrations are the copyright of maranGraphics, Inc.

U.S. Corporate Sales	U.S. Trade Sales
Contact maranGraphics at (800) 469-6616 or fax (905) 890-9434.	Contact IDG Books at (800) 434-3422 or (650) 655-3000.

ABOUT IDG BOOKS WORLDWIDE

Welcome to the world of IDG Books Worldwide.

IDG Books Worldwide, Inc., is a subsidiary of International Data Group, the world's largest publisher of computer-related information and the leading global provider of information services on information technology. IDG was founded more than 30 years ago by Patrick J. McGovern and now employs more than 9,000 people worldwide. IDG publishes more than 290 computer publications in over 75 countries. More than 90 million people read one or more IDG publications each month.

Launched in 1990, IDG Books Worldwide is today the #1 publisher of best-selling computer books in the United States. We are proud to have received eight awards from the Computer Press Association in recognition of editorial excellence and three from Computer Currents' First Annual Readers' Choice Awards. Our best-selling ...For Dummies® series has more than 50 million copies in print with translations in 31 languages. IDG Books Worldwide, through a joint venture with IDG's Hi-Tech Beijing, became the first U.S. publisher to publish a computer book in the People's Republic of China. In record time, IDG Books Worldwide has become the first choice for millions of readers around the world who want to learn how to better manage their businesses.

Our mission is simple: Every one of our books is designed to bring extra value and skill-building instructions to the reader. Our books are written by experts who understand and care about our readers. The knowledge base of our editorial staff comes from years of experience in publishing, education, and journalism — experience we use to produce books to carry us into the new millennium. In short, we care about books, so we attract the best people. We devote special attention to details such as audience, interior design, use of icons, and illustrations. And because we use an efficient process of authoring, editing, and desktop publishing our books electronically, we can spend more time ensuring superior content and less time on the technicalities of making books.

You can count on our commitment to deliver high-quality books at competitive prices on topics you want to read about. At IDG Books Worldwide, we continue in the IDG tradition of delivering quality for more than 30 years. You'll find no better book on a subject than one from IDG Books Worldwide.

John Kilcullen
Chairman and CEO
IDG Books Worldwide, Inc.

Steven Berkowitz
President and Publisher
IDG Books Worldwide, Inc.

Eighth Annual Computer Press Awards 1992

Ninth Annual Computer Press Awards 1993

Tenth Annual Computer Press Awards 1994

Eleventh Annual Computer Press Awards 1995

IDG is the world's leading IT media, research and exposition company. Founded in 1964, IDG had 1997 revenues of $2.05 billion and has more than 9,000 employees worldwide. IDG offers the widest range of media options that reach IT buyers in 75 countries representing 95% of worldwide IT spending. IDG's diverse product and services portfolio spans six key areas including print publishing, online publishing, expositions and conferences, market research, education and training, and global marketing services. More than 90 million people read one or more of IDG's 290 magazines and newspapers, including IDG's leading global brands — Computerworld, PC World, Network World, Macworld and the Channel World family of publications. IDG Books Worldwide is one of the fastest-growing computer book publishers in the world, with more than 700 titles in 36 languages. The "...For Dummies®" series alone has more than 50 million copies in print. IDG offers online users the largest network of technology-specific Web sites around the world through IDG.net (http://www.idg.net), which comprises more than 225 targeted Web sites in 55 countries worldwide. International Data Corporation (IDC) is the world's largest provider of information technology data, analysis and consulting, with research centers in over 41 countries and more than 400 research analysts worldwide. IDG World Expo is a leading producer of more than 168 globally branded conferences and expositions in 35 countries including E3 (Electronic Entertainment Expo), Macworld Expo, ComNet, Windows World Expo, ICE (Internet Commerce Expo), Agenda, DEMO, and Spotlight. IDG's training subsidiary, ExecuTrain, is the world's largest computer training company, with more than 230 locations worldwide and 785 training courses. IDG Marketing Services helps industry-leading IT companies build international brand recognition by developing global integrated marketing programs via IDG's print, online and exposition products worldwide. Further information about the company can be found at www.idg.com. 1/24/99

maranGraphics is a family-run business located near Toronto, Canada.

At **maranGraphics**, we believe in producing great computer books–one book at a time.

Each maranGraphics book uses the award-winning communication process that we have been developing over the last 25 years. Using this process, we organize screen shots, text and illustrations in a way that makes it easy for you to learn new concepts and tasks.

We spend hours deciding the best way to perform each task, so you don't have to! Our clear, easy-to-follow screen shots and instructions walk you through each task from beginning to end.

Our detailed illustrations go hand-in-hand with the text to help reinforce the information. Each illustration is a labor of love–some take up to a week to draw!

We want to thank you for purchasing what we feel are the best computer books money can buy. We hope you enjoy using this book as much as we enjoyed creating it!

Sincerely,

The Maran Family

Please visit us on the Web at:
www.maran.com

Credits

Author:
Ruth Maran

Technical Consultant:
Paul Whitehead

Copy Editors:
Cathy Benn
Jill Maran

Project Manager:
Judy Maran

Editing & Screen Captures:
Raquel Scott
Janice Boyer
Michelle Kirchner
James Menzies
Frances Lea
Stacey Morrison

Layout & Illustrations:
Treena Lees

Illustrators:
Russ Marini
Jamie Bell
Peter Grecco
Sean Johannesen
Steven Schaerer

Screens & Illustrations:
Jimmy Tam

Indexer:
Raquel Scott

Permissions Coordinator:
Jenn Hillman

Post Production:
Robert Maran

Editorial Support:
Barry Pruett
Martine Edwards

Acknowledgments

Thanks to the dedicated staff of maranGraphics, including
Jamie Bell, Cathy Benn, Janice Boyer, Peter Grecco,
Jenn Hillman, Sean Johannesen, Michelle Kirchner,
Wanda Lawrie, Frances Lea, Treena Lees, Jill Maran, Judy Maran,
Robert Maran, Sherry Maran, Russ Marini, James Menzies,
Stacey Morrison, Steven Schaerer, Raquel Scott, Jimmy Tam,
Roxanne Van Damme, Paul Whitehead and Kelleigh Wing.

Finally, to Richard Maran who originated the easy-to-use
graphic format of this guide. Thank you for your
inspiration and guidance.

Table of Contents

Table of Contents

CHAPTER 11

USING STYLE SHEETS

CHAPTER 12

PUBLISH WEB PAGES

CHAPTER 13

SUMMARY OF HTML TAGS

CHAPTER 1

THE INTERNET

Are you curious about the Internet? Read this chapter to learn about the Internet and what it has to offer.

INTRODUCTION TO THE INTERNET

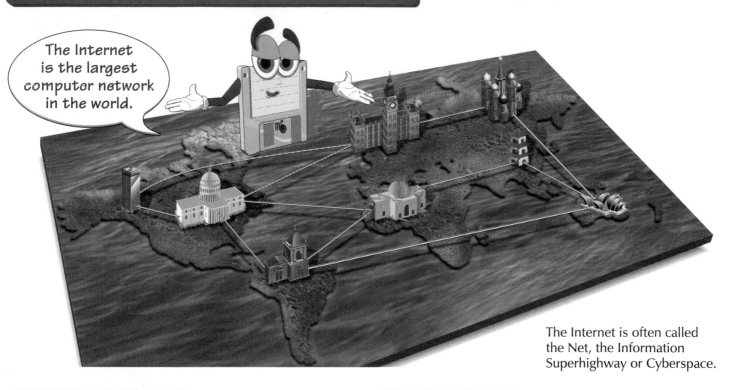

The Internet is the largest computer network in the world.

The Internet is often called the Net, the Information Superhighway or Cyberspace.

HISTORY OF THE INTERNET

In the late 1960s, the U.S. Defense Department began the Internet as a military research project. The government created a network that covered a large geographic area and that could withstand a nuclear attack. If part of the network failed, information could find a new route around the disabled computers.

The network quickly grew to include scientists and researchers across the country and eventually included schools, businesses, organizations and individuals around the world.

STRUCTURE OF THE INTERNET

The Internet consists of thousands of connected networks around the world. A network is a collection of computers that are connected to share information. Each government agency, company and organization on the Internet is responsible for maintaining its own network on the Internet.

ELECTRONIC MAIL

Electronic mail (e-mail) is the most popular feature on the Internet. You can exchange electronic mail with people around the world, including friends, family members, colleagues, customers and even people you meet on the Internet. Electronic mail is fast, easy, inexpensive and saves paper.

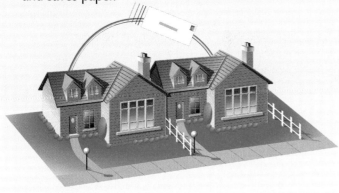

INFORMATION AND ENTERTAINMENT

The Internet gives you access to information on every subject imaginable. You can review newspapers, magazines, academic papers, government documents, television show transcripts, famous speeches, recipes, job listings and airline schedules. You can also play games, watch videos, listen to music and chat with people around the world.

ONLINE SHOPPING

You can order products on the Internet without leaving your home. You can purchase items such as books, computer programs, flowers, music CDs, pizza, stocks and used cars.

DISCUSSION GROUPS

You can join discussion groups to meet people with similar interests around the world. You can ask questions and discuss issues on topics such as food, pets, music, politics and sports. Usenet newsgroups are the most popular discussion groups on the Internet. You can also find discussion groups on many Web sites.

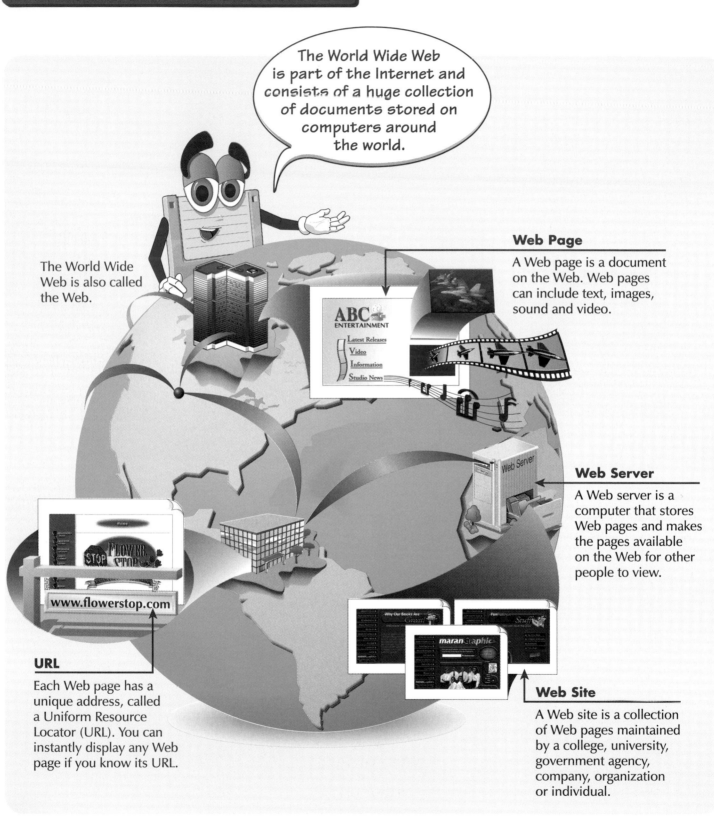

The World Wide Web is part of the Internet and consists of a huge collection of documents stored on computers around the world.

The World Wide Web is also called the Web.

Web Page

A Web page is a document on the Web. Web pages can include text, images, sound and video.

Web Server

A Web server is a computer that stores Web pages and makes the pages available on the Web for other people to view.

www.flowerstop.com

URL

Each Web page has a unique address, called a Uniform Resource Locator (URL). You can instantly display any Web page if you know its URL.

Web Site

A Web site is a collection of Web pages maintained by a college, university, government agency, company, organization or individual.

HYPERLINKS

Web pages contain hyperlinks. Hyperlinks are highlighted text or images on a Web page that connect to other pages on the Web. You can select a hyperlink to display a Web page located on the same computer or on a computer across the city, country or world. Hyperlinks allow you to easily navigate through a vast amount of information by jumping from one Web page to another. Hyperlinks are also known as links.

WEB BROWSERS

A Web browser is a program that allows you to view and explore information on the Web.

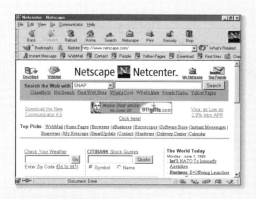

Microsoft Internet Explorer

Microsoft Internet Explorer is a popular Web browser that comes with Windows 98. You can also obtain Microsoft Internet Explorer at the www.microsoft.com/ie Web site or at computer stores.

Netscape Navigator

Netscape Navigator is a popular Web browser that you can obtain at the www.netscape.com Web site or at computer stores.

TYPES OF CONNECTIONS

MODEM

Most people use a modem to connect to the Internet through a regular telephone line. A modem with a speed of 56 Kbps is recommended for browsing the Web. Slower modems will take longer to display information on a screen.

ISDN

An Integrated Services Digital Network (ISDN) line is a digital phone line offered by telephone companies in most cities. An ISDN line can transfer information at speeds from 56 Kbps to 128 Kbps.

CABLE MODEM

A cable modem allows you to connect to the Internet with the same cable that attaches to a television set. A cable modem can transfer information at a speed of up to 3,000 Kbps. You can contact your local cable company to determine if they offer cable Internet services.

DSL

Digital Subscriber Line (DSL) is a service offered by telephone companies in many cities. DSL can transfer information at speeds from 1,000 Kbps to 6,000 Kbps.

HOW TO CONNECT

INTERNET SERVICE PROVIDER

An Internet Service Provider (ISP) is a company that offers access to the Internet. Most ISPs offer a certain number of hours on the Internet each month for a set fee. If you exceed the total number of hours, you are usually charged for every extra hour that you use the Internet. Some ISPs offer unlimited access to the Internet for a set fee.

COMMERCIAL ONLINE SERVICE

A commercial online service is a company that offers access to the Internet and provides well-organized information and services such as daily news, weather reports, encyclopedias and chat rooms. Popular commercial online services include America Online and The Microsoft Network.

Most commercial online services offer a certain number of hours each month for a set fee. If you exceed the total number of hours, you are usually charged for every extra hour that you use the service.

UNIVERSITY OR COMPANY

Universities and colleges often provide students and teachers with free access to the Internet. Many companies also provide free Internet access for their employees.

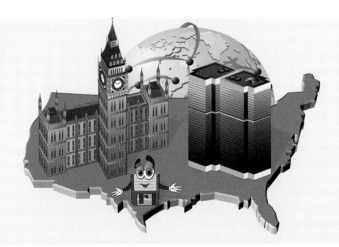

mG's WEB PAGE

- About mG
- Current Issues
- What's New
- Free Services

mG

World Wide Web

CHAPTER 2

INTRODUCTION TO CREATING WEB PAGES

Are you thinking about creating Web pages? This chapter will outline some important considerations.

REASONS FOR CREATING WEB PAGES

PERSONAL

SHARE PERSONAL INFORMATION

Many people create Web pages to share information about their families, pets, vacations or favorite hobbies. Some people create Web pages to present a résumé to potential employers.

SHARE KNOWLEDGE

Many scientists and business professionals make their work available on the Web. If you are experienced in an area that many people are unfamiliar with, you can create Web pages to share your knowledge.

ENTERTAIN READERS

Many people create Web pages to display collections of jokes or humorous stories. You can also create Web pages to display information, pictures, sound clips and videos about a favorite celebrity, sports team or TV show.

PROMOTE INTERESTS

You can create Web pages to display information about an organization or club that you belong to. You can include a schedule of upcoming events and detailed information about the goals of the organization.

COMMERCIAL

PROVIDE INFORMATION

Companies often place pages on the Web to provide information about their company and the products and services they offer. Companies can use Web pages to keep the public informed about new products and interesting news. Many companies display their press releases on the Web.

SHOPPING

Many companies create Web pages that allow readers to order products and services over the Internet. Companies can display descriptions and pictures of products to help readers determine which products they want to purchase.

JOB LISTINGS

Many companies use Web pages to advertise jobs that are available within the company. Some companies allow readers to submit résumés through their Web site.

CONTACT INFORMATION

Companies can display their office addresses and phone numbers on their Web pages. This helps readers contact the company to ask questions and express opinions.

STEPS FOR CREATING WEB PAGES

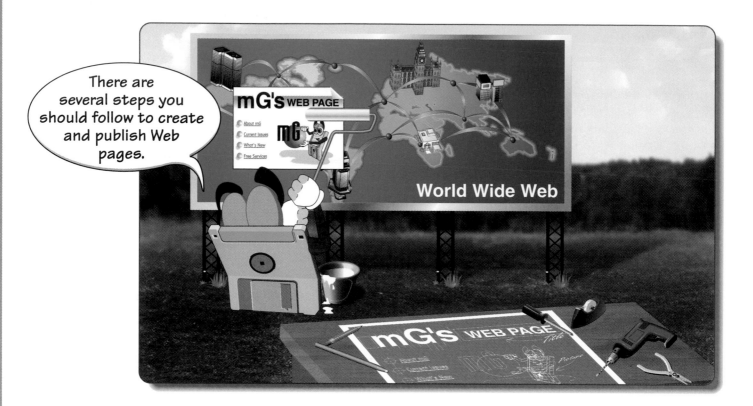

There are several steps you should follow to create and publish Web pages.

STEP 1—PLAN YOUR WEB PAGES

Decide what you want to accomplish with your Web pages. Decide on a main topic or theme for your Web pages and then determine the type of information you want to include.

STEP 2—GATHER INFORMATION

Collect the information you want to include on your Web pages, such as text, images, diagrams and contact numbers. Make sure the information you gather directly relates to the main topic or theme you chose for your Web pages.

STEP 3—ORGANIZE INFORMATION

Divide the information you gathered into sections. Each section should be a separate Web page. Each Web page should discuss a different concept or idea and should contain enough information to fill a single screen.

STEP 4—ENTER TEXT

Enter the text you want to appear on your Web pages in a text editor or word processor. Each Web page should be a separate document. You can then add HyperText Markup Language (HTML) tags to the text to convert the documents into Web pages.

STEP 5—ADD IMAGES

You can add images to enhance the appearance of your Web pages. You can create your own images, use a scanner to scan images into your computer, buy images at computer stores or find images on the Internet.

STEP 6—ADD LINKS

You can add links to your Web pages. Links are text or images that readers can select to display other pages on the Web. Links allow readers to easily move through information of interest.

STEP 7—PUBLISH WEB PAGES

When you finish creating your Web pages, you can transfer the pages to a computer that makes pages available on the Web. You should then test the Web pages to ensure your links work properly and your information appears the way you want.

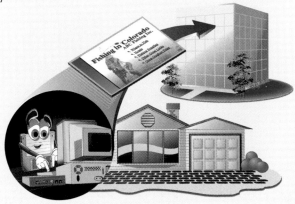

When creating Web pages, you should carefully consider the content of the pages.

EXAMINE YOUR FAVORITE WEB PAGES

Before you start creating your Web pages, take a close look at some of your favorite Web pages. Determine what you like about the Web pages and consider how you can use these ideas on your pages.

You can find a list of great Web pages at:

www.zdnet.com/pcmag/special/web100

PROOFREAD INFORMATION

Carefully check your Web pages for spelling and grammar errors. Spelling mistakes will make readers think that you are careless and that your Web pages are inaccurate. You may want to print your Web pages to help you proofread the pages.

PUT IMPORTANT INFORMATION FIRST

Always display the most important information at the top of each Web page. Some readers will not scroll through a Web page to read all the information. These readers will miss important information if you do not display the information at the top of each page.

EMPHASIZE IMPORTANT INFORMATION

If some parts of your Web page are more important than others, use the available formatting features to make the information stand out. Do not bury important ideas or concepts in long paragraphs.

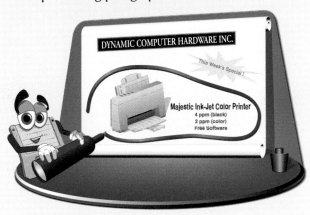

PAGE LENGTH

Web pages should not be too short or too long. If a Web page is shorter than half a screen of information, try to combine the information with another page. If a Web page is longer than five screens, try to break up the page into several shorter pages.

AVOID "UNDER CONSTRUCTION" LABELS

You should avoid using "under construction" labels for Web pages that are not complete. You will frustrate readers when they visit a Web page that does not contain useful information. Do not make your Web pages available on the Web until the pages are complete.

PROVIDE A FAQ

A FAQ is a list of Frequently Asked Questions about a topic. A FAQ can help answer questions that people have about your Web pages and can help prevent people from sending you e-mail messages asking the same questions over and over again.

COPYRIGHT CONSIDERATIONS

If you plan to use information or images you did not create, make sure the information or images are not copyrighted. Many pages on the Web offer information and images that do not have copyright restrictions.

AVOID SPECIFIC WEB BROWSER INSTRUCTIONS

Avoid giving detailed instructions on how to perform tasks using a specific Web browser. People who use a different Web browser may not be able to perform the task using the instructions you provide.

USE WARNINGS

If your Web pages display information that some readers may consider offensive, place a warning on your main page. When readers visit your Web site, they will see the warning and can then decide whether they want to view your pages.

UPDATE INFORMATION

You should update your Web pages on a regular basis. If the information on your Web pages never changes, people will only read the pages once and will not revisit them in the future. You should include the date on your Web pages to let readers know when you last updated the pages.

USE HEADINGS

Always use headings to emphasize your titles and subtitles. Headings allow readers to glance through a Web page and quickly find information of interest without having to read the entire page.

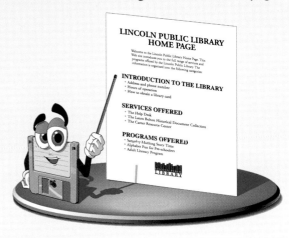

INCLUDE CONTACT INFORMATION

Always include your name and e-mail address on Web pages you create. This allows readers to contact you if they have questions or comments.

TRANSFER SPEED

When creating your Web pages, try to keep the file size of the pages and images as small as possible. This will speed up the display of your Web pages by reducing the time it takes for the information to transfer.

WEB PAGES WITHOUT IMAGES

Some people turn off the display of images to browse the Web more quickly, while others use Web browsers that cannot display images. Always design your Web pages so that readers who do not see images will still get valuable information from your pages.

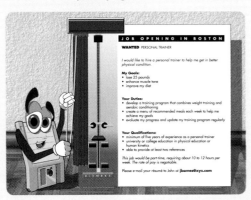

The home page is the main Web page in a Web site. The home page is usually the first page people see when they visit a Web site.

The home page is usually named index.html or index.htm. You should check with the company that makes your Web pages available on the Web to determine what name to use.

SUMMARY

Always include a brief summary of your Web pages on the home page. You should state whether the purpose of your Web pages is to entertain or inform readers. You should not assume that readers will understand the purpose of your Web pages just by reading the title.

TABLE OF CONTENTS

Your home page should include a table of contents that lists the information contained in your Web site. You should include links that allow readers to quickly access information of interest.

BOOKMARK REMINDER

Web browsers have a feature called bookmarks or favorites that allows people to store the addresses of Web pages they visit. You can include an image or phrase on your home page to remind readers to bookmark your Web page. This allows readers to quickly return to your Web site.

The layout of your Web pages depends on the type of information your pages contain and the way the pages relate to each other.

LINEAR

A linear layout organizes Web pages in a straight line. This layout is ideal for Web pages that people should read in a specific order, such as pages containing a story or step-by-step instructions.

HIERARCHICAL

In a hierarchical layout, all Web pages branch off a main page. The main Web page provides the most general information, while the other pages provide more specific information.

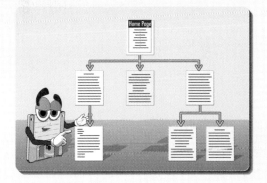

WEB

A Web layout has no overall structure. This type of layout is ideal for Web pages that people do not need to read in a specific order. Readers can easily move from one Web page to another.

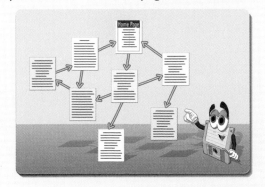

COMBINATION

A combination of layouts provides readers with the greatest amount of flexibility when reading your Web pages. For example, you can use both a hierarchical and Web layout for your Web pages.

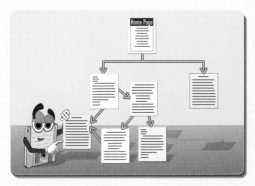

HyperText Markup Language (HTML) is a computer language used to create Web pages.

HTML DOCUMENTS

Web pages are HTML documents. An HTML document consists of text and special instructions, called tags. HTML documents have the .html or .htm extension (example: index.html).

A Web browser interprets the tags in an HTML document and displays the document as a Web page.

HTML ADVANTAGES

An HTML document can be displayed on any type of computer, such as a Macintosh or IBM-compatible computer. This means that you do not have to create different HTML documents for different types of computers. Since HTML documents contain only text, they transfer quickly over the Web.

HTML VERSIONS

There are several versions of HTML. Each version offers new features to give people more control when creating Web pages. HTML version 4.0 is the latest version of HTML.

Some companies that make Web browsers, such as Netscape and Microsoft, have developed their own tags that Web browsers made by other companies may not be able to understand. If a Web browser does not understand a tag, the tag is usually ignored.

WORK WITH TAGS

TAGS

Each tag gives a specific instruction and is surrounded by angle brackets < >. Most tags have an opening tag and a closing tag that affect the text between the tags. The closing tag has a forward slash (/). Some tags have only an opening tag.

You can use uppercase or lowercase letters when typing tags. Most people type tags in uppercase letters to make the tags stand out from the main text.

ATTRIBUTES

Some tags have attributes that offer options for the tag. For example, the <FONT> tag has a COLOR attribute that lets you change the color of text.

WEB PAGE STRUCTURE

Tags tell a Web browser about the structure of a Web page, but do not specifically define how to display the Web page. Each Web browser may interpret HTML tags differently, so a Web page may not look the same when displayed in different Web browsers.

VIEW HTML TAGS

When you find a Web page that you like, you can use your Web browser to view the HTML tags the author used to create the Web page. This is a great way to get ideas for creating your own Web pages.

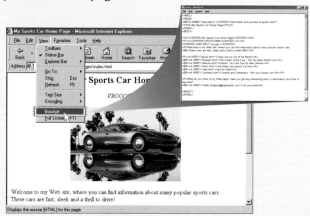

PROGRAMS FOR CREATING WEB PAGES

You can choose between several types of programs to create Web pages.

TEXT EDITOR OR WORD PROCESSOR

Text Editor

A text editor is a simple program you can use to create and edit documents that contain only text. Text editors do not include advanced editing and formatting features. Popular text editors include Notepad for Windows and SimpleText for the Macintosh.

Word Processor

A word processor is a program that provides advanced editing and formatting features to help you create documents. Any formatting you apply to text will not appear when you view documents you create on the Web. Popular word processors include Microsoft Word and Corel WordPerfect.

To create a Web page using a text editor or word processor, you must type the text for the Web page and then add HTML tags to specify how you want the text to appear on the Web page. You need a Web browser to see how the Web page will appear on the Web.

Many word processors allow you to convert documents you create into Web pages. This lets you create Web pages without having to know HTML.

HTML EDITOR

An HTML editor is a program you can use to create Web pages. HTML editors offer menus and toolbars that you can use to add HTML tags to your Web pages. Many HTML editors include a validator that can check your Web pages for HTML errors. You need to know HTML to create a Web page using an HTML editor.

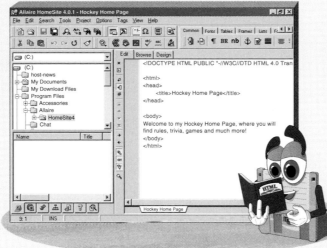

Some HTML editors allow you to see how Web pages you create will appear on the Web, while others require you to use a Web browser to view your Web pages.

You can obtain HTML editors at the following Web sites:

BBEdit
www.barebones.com

HomeSite
www.allaire.com

VISUAL EDITOR

A visual editor is a program you can use to graphically create Web pages. Visual editors enter HTML tags for you as you create a Web page. You do not need to know HTML to create a Web page using a visual editor.

Visual editors hide HTML tags from view, so you can see how your Web pages will look as you create the Web pages.

You can obtain visual editors at the following Web sites:

HoTMetaL PRO
www.softquad.com

Microsoft FrontPage
www.microsoft.com/frontpage

Fruit & Flowers, I...

Grow beautiful, exotic flowers and impress...
Grow your own fruit and save on your groc...

Our fruit selection includes:
• Popular berries such as strawberries, rasp...
  and blueberries
• Exotic fruit such as mangos, papayas and...

Our flower selection includes:
• Seasonal plants such as poinsettias, holly a...
  mistletoe
• Tropical flowers such as orchids, birds of p...
  and yellow jasmine

Fruit & Flowers Guarantee:
Our fruit and flowers are guaranteed for one year. If you are not satisfied in a...
with our products, simply return them to us for a full, unconditional ref...

‹HEAD› **Golf Tournaments**

‹BODY› ...interested in competing in any tournaments, ...se register as soon as possible. The following golf tournaments will be taking place this summer at the Green Haven Golf Course:

• June 26:   Celebrity Classic
• July 3:   Annual Trophy Tournament
• July18:   Charity Golf Tournament
• August 7:   Amateur Tourney
• August 21:   Golfer's Annual
• August 28:   Club Championships

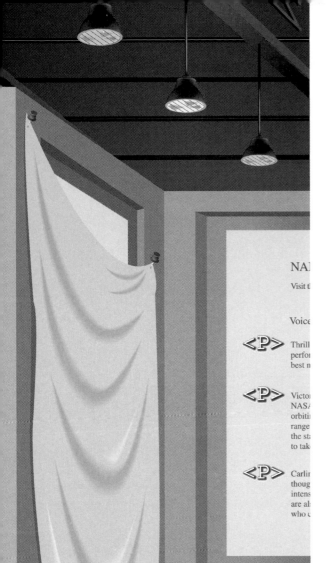

CHAPTER 3

GETTING STARTED

Are you ready to begin creating Web pages? This chapter will provide you with the basics you need to get started.

SET UP A WEB PAGE

You can create a Web page using a word processor or text editor.

For information on word processors and text editors, see page 24.

SET UP A WEB PAGE

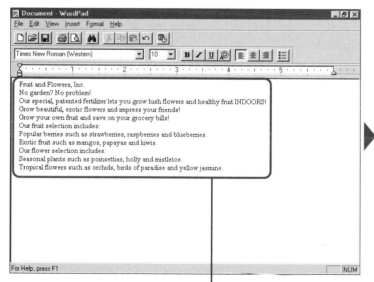

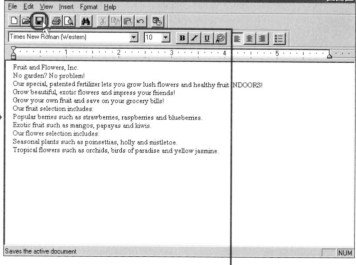

1 Start the word processor or text editor you will use to create a Web page. In this example, we started Microsoft WordPad.

2 Type the text you want to appear on the Web page.

■ Do not format the text. You must use HTML tags to format the text.

3 Check the Web page for spelling and grammar errors.

4 Click 🖫 to save the Web page.

■ The Save As dialog box appears.

28

Why does the text scroll off my screen?

When you type text in a text editor or simple word processor, the text may scroll off the screen. When you view the document in a Web browser, the text will fit properly on the screen. You can choose to wrap text in a text editor or word processor.

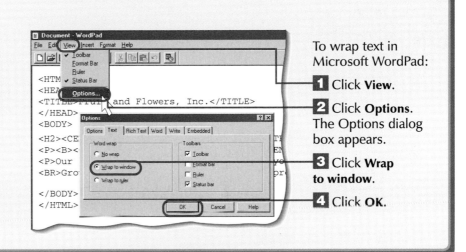

To wrap text in Microsoft WordPad:

1 Click **View**.

2 Click **Options**. The Options dialog box appears.

3 Click **Wrap to window**.

4 Click **OK**.

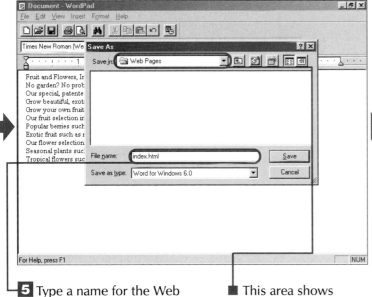

5 Type a name for the Web page. Make sure you add the **.html** or **.htm** extension to the Web page name.

Note: A Web page name can contain letters and numbers, but no spaces. The main Web page is usually named ***index.html***.

■ This area shows the location where the program will store the Web page. You can click this area to change the location.

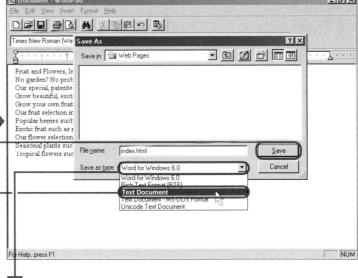

6 Click this area to list the ways you can save the Web page.

7 Click **Text Document**.

8 Click **Save**.

■ A dialog box will appear, stating that all formatting will be removed from the Web page. Click **Yes** to save the Web page.

CONTINUED

There are some basic HTML tags you must add to every Web page you create.

SET UP A WEB PAGE (CONTINUED)

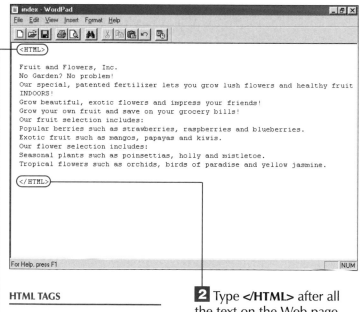

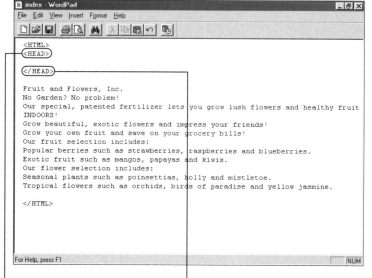

HTML TAGS

You need to identify a document as a Web page.

1 Type **<HTML>** before all the text on the Web page.

2 Type **</HTML>** after all the text on the Web page.

■ Although Web browsers can display a Web page without the HTML tags, it is considered proper form to include these tags.

HEAD TAGS

The head contains information about a Web page, such as the title.

1 Type **<HEAD>** directly below the <HTML> tag.

2 Press the Enter key twice.

3 Type **</HEAD>**.

■ Although Web browsers can display a Web page without the HEAD tags, it is considered proper form to include these tags.

TIP

What title should I use for my Web page?

You should choose a brief, descriptive title that will interest people in reading your Web page. Use a title such as "Golf Tournaments" rather than a less descriptive title such as "Chapter Two" or "My Home Page."

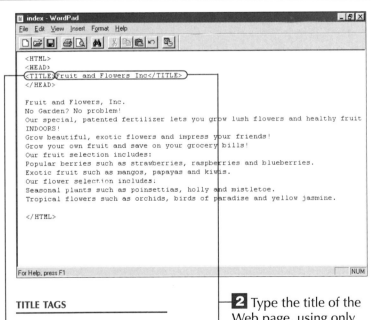

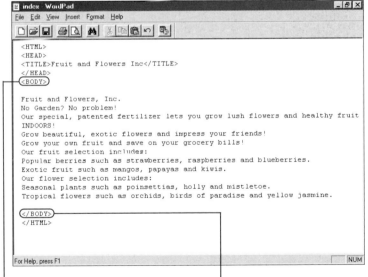

TITLE TAGS

You must give a Web page a title that describes its contents. The title usually appears in the title bar of a Web browser window.

1 Type **<TITLE>** directly below the <HEAD> tag.

2 Type the title of the Web page, using only letters and numbers (A to Z and 0 to 9).

3 Type **</TITLE>**.

BODY TAGS

You must place the BODY tags around the contents of a Web page.

1 Type **<BODY>** directly below the </HEAD> tag.

2 Type **</BODY>** directly above the </HTML> tag.

You can display your Web page in a Web browser. This allows you to see how your Web page will appear on the Web.

To display a Web page in a Web browser, you need a Web browser program such as Microsoft Internet Explorer or Netscape Navigator. For information on where you can obtain a Web browser program, see page 7.

DISPLAY WEB PAGE IN WEB BROWSER

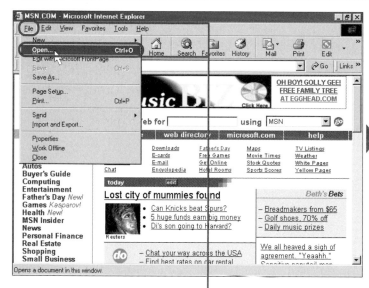

1 Start the Web browser you want to use to display your Web page. In this example, we started Microsoft Internet Explorer.

2 To open your Web page in the Web browser, click **File**.

3 Click **Open**.

■ The Open dialog box appears.

4 Click **Browse** to locate the Web page on your computer.

*Note: If you are using Netscape Navigator, click **Choose File**.*

■ The Microsoft Internet Explorer dialog box appears.

TIP

Should I display my Web page in more than one Web browser?

Yes. You should display your Web page in several Web browsers so you can see how each browser will display your Web page. Each Web browser will display your Web page in a slightly different way. The most popular Web browsers are Microsoft Internet Explorer and Netscape Navigator.

Microsoft Internet Explorer

Netscape Navigator

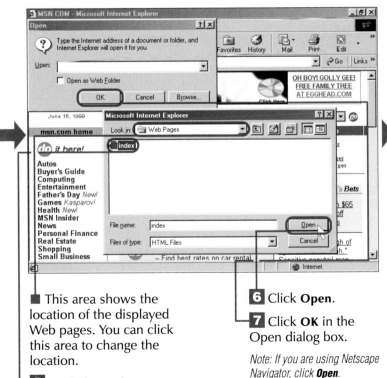

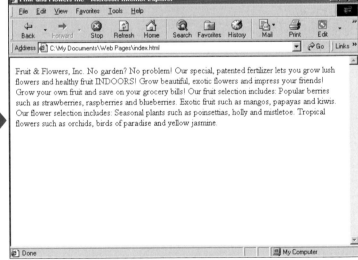

■ This area shows the location of the displayed Web pages. You can click this area to change the location.

5 Click the Web page you want to open.

6 Click **Open**.

7 Click **OK** in the Open dialog box.

*Note: If you are using Netscape Navigator, click **Open**.*

■ The Web page appears in the Web browser.

■ If you later make changes to the Web page, you can display the updated page in the Web browser. To display changes you make to a Web page in a Web browser, see page 34.

DISPLAY WEB PAGE CHANGES IN WEB BROWSER

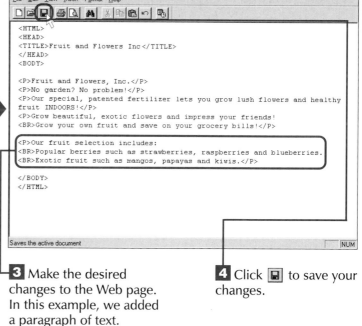

> If you make changes to your Web page, you can display the changes in a Web browser to see how the updated page will appear on the Web.

DISPLAY WEB PAGE CHANGES IN WEB BROWSER

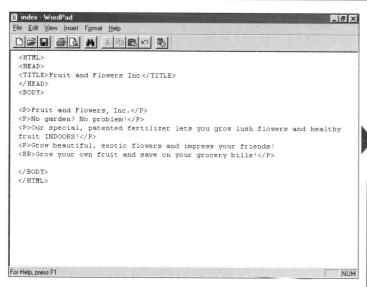

CHANGE A WEB PAGE

1 Start the program you used to create your Web page. In this example, we started Microsoft WordPad.

2 Open the Web page you want to change.

3 Make the desired changes to the Web page. In this example, we added a paragraph of text.

4 Click 🖫 to save your changes.

Can other people view my Web page?

Even though you can display your Web page in a Web browser, other people on the Web cannot view your Web page. When you complete your Web page, you must transfer the page to a company that makes Web pages available on the Web before other people can view the page. For information on companies that make Web pages available on the Web, see page 192.

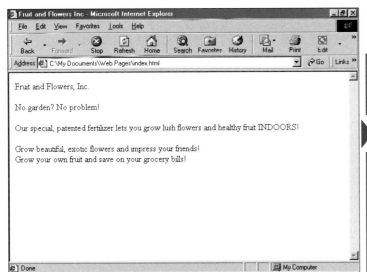

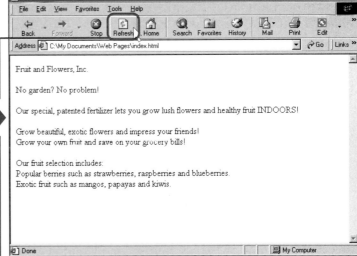

DISPLAY CHANGES IN WEB BROWSER

1 Display the Web page in a Web browser. To display a Web page in a Web browser, see page 32.

2 Click **Refresh** to display your changes in the Web browser.

*Note: If you are using Netscape Navigator, click **Reload**.*

When creating a Web page, you must specify where you want each paragraph to begin.

START A NEW PARAGRAPH

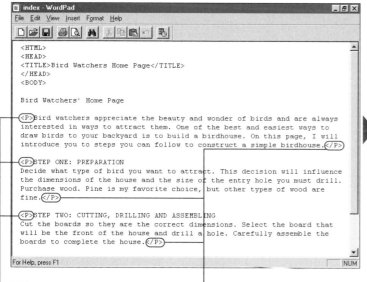

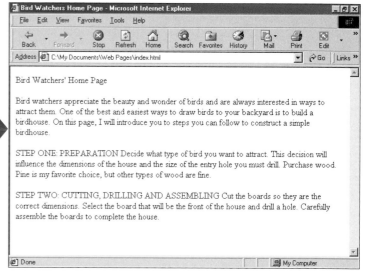

1 Type **<P>** in front of each paragraph on your Web page.

2 Type **</P>** after each paragraph on your Web page.

■ The Web browser displays a blank line between each paragraph.

■ To display your Web page in a Web browser, see pages 32 to 35.

What determines the width of the paragraphs on my Web page?

The width of your paragraphs depends on the width of the Web browser window. If a reader changes the size of a Web browser window, the width of the paragraphs will also change. This ensures that a reader will always see all the text in the paragraphs on the screen.

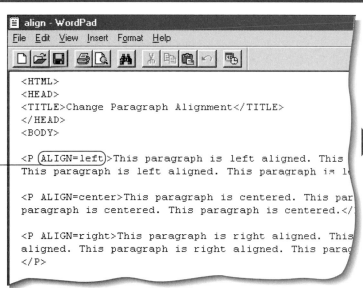

```
<HTML>
<HEAD>
<TITLE>Change Paragraph Alignment</TITLE>
</HEAD>
<BODY>

<P ALIGN=left>This paragraph is left aligned. This
This paragraph is left aligned. This paragraph is l

<P ALIGN=center>This paragraph is centered. This par
paragraph is centered. This paragraph is centered.</

<P ALIGN=right>This paragraph is right aligned. This
aligned. This paragraph is right aligned. This parag
</P>
```

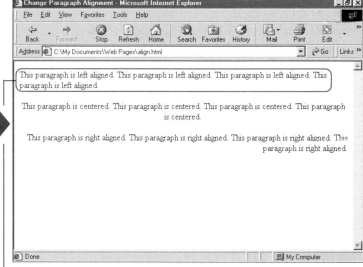

CHANGE PARAGRAPH ALIGNMENT

1 In the <P> tag for the paragraph you want to change, type **ALIGN=?** replacing **?** with the way you want to align the paragraph (**left**, **center** or **right**).

■ The Web browser displays the paragraph with the alignment you selected.

■ To display your Web page in a Web browser, see pages 32 to 35.

Note: The ALIGN attribute is still supported by Web browsers, but the use of style sheets is now preferred. For information on style sheets, see page 172.

When creating a Web page, you must specify where you want each new line of text to begin.

Starting a new line is useful for separating short lines of text, such as text in a mailing address or poem.

START A NEW LINE

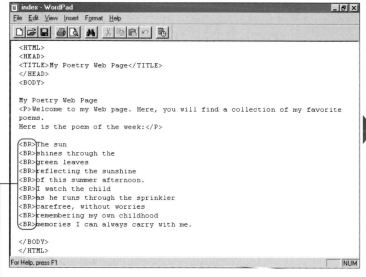

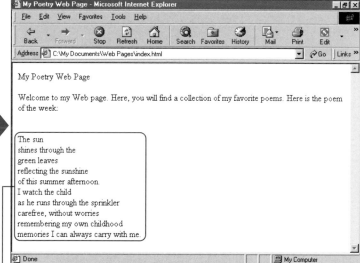

1 Type **
** in front of each line of text you want to appear on its own line.

■ The Web browser displays each line of text on its own line.

■ To display your Web page in a Web browser, see pages 32 to 35.

You can center text on your Web page. Centering text can help you emphasize important information.

You should only center short phrases since long paragraphs can be difficult to read when centered.

CENTER TEXT

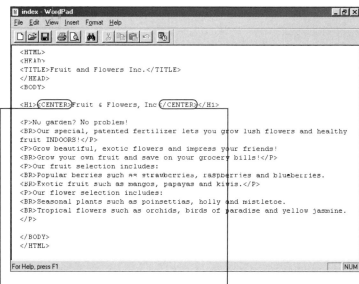

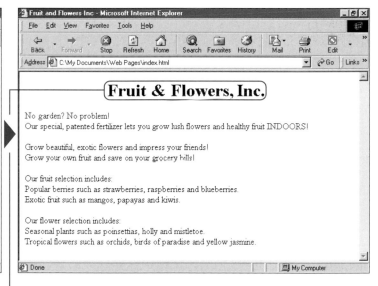

1 Type **<CENTER>** in front of the text you want to center.

2 Type **</CENTER>** after the text you want to center.

■ The Web browser centers the text.

■ To display your Web page in a Web browser, see pages 32 to 35.

Note: The CENTER tag is still supported by Web browsers, but the use of style sheets is now preferred. For information on style sheets, see page 172.

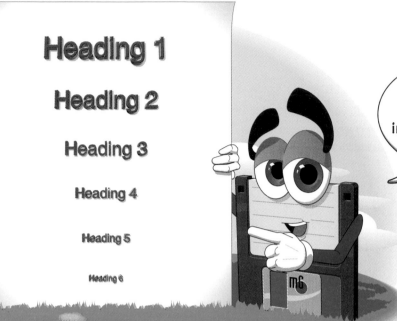

You can use headings to help organize the information on your Web page.

There are six heading levels you can use. You should avoid using more than three different heading levels on a single Web page.

ADD A HEADING

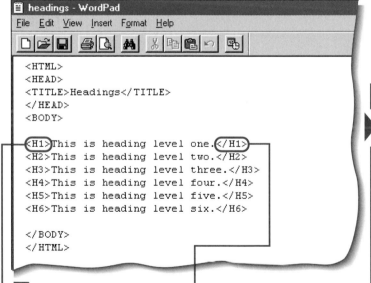

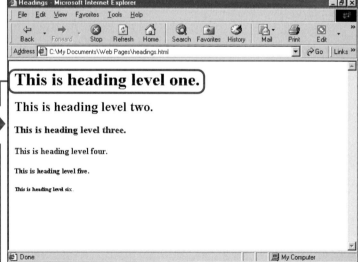

1 Type **<H?>** in front of the text you want to make a heading. Replace **?** with the number of the heading level you want to use, from 1 to 6.

Note: For information on the heading levels, see the top of page 41.

2 Type **</H?>** after the text you want to make a heading. Replace **?** with the number you used in step **1**.

■ The Web browser displays the heading.

■ To display your Web page in a Web browser, see pages 32 to 35.

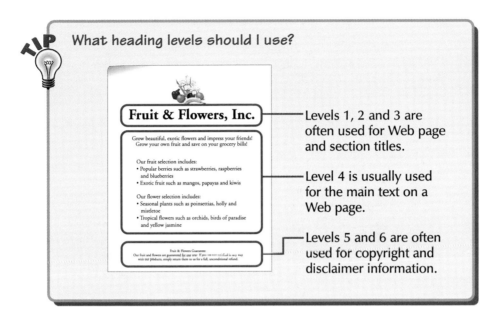

TIP

What heading levels should I use?

Levels 1, 2 and 3 are often used for Web page and section titles.

Level 4 is usually used for the main text on a Web page.

Levels 5 and 6 are often used for copyright and disclaimer information.

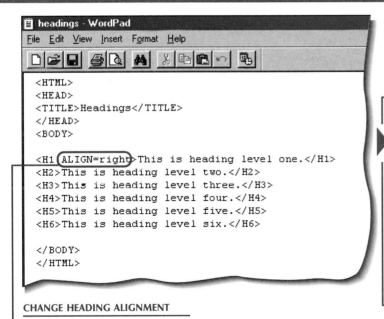

```
<HTML>
<HEAD>
<TITLE>Headings</TITLE>
</HEAD>
<BODY>

<H1 ALIGN=right>This is heading level one.</H1>
<H2>This is heading level two.</H2>
<H3>This is heading level three.</H3>
<H4>This is heading level four.</H4>
<H5>This is heading level five.</H5>
<H6>This is heading level six.</H6>

</BODY>
</HTML>
```

CHANGE HEADING ALIGNMENT

1 In the **<H?>** tag for the heading you want to change, type **ALIGN=?** replacing **?** with the way you want to align the heading (**left**, **center** or **right**).

■ The Web browser displays the heading with the alignment you selected.

■ To display your Web page in a Web browser, see pages 32 to 35.

Note: The ALIGN attribute is still supported by Web browsers, but the use of style sheets is now preferred. For information on style sheets, see page 172.

USING PREFORMATTED TEXT

A Web browser usually ignores blank lines and extra spaces you add when typing the text for your Web page. You can use tags to retain the spacing of text you type.

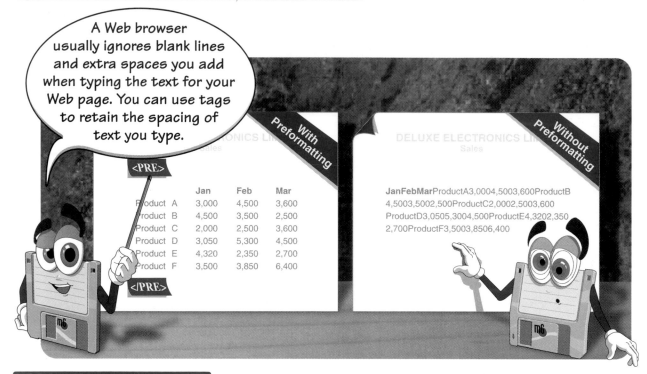

With Preformatting

	Jan	Feb	Mar
Product A	3,000	4,500	3,600
Product B	4,500	3,500	2,500
Product C	2,000	2,500	3,600
Product D	3,050	5,300	4,500
Product E	4,320	2,350	2,700
Product F	3,500	3,850	6,400

Without Preformatting

JanFebMarProductA3,0004,5003,600ProductB 4,5003,5002,500ProductC2,0002,5003,600 ProductD3,0505,3004,500ProductE4,3202,350 2,700ProductF3,5003,8506,400

Preformatted text is useful for creating a simple table.

USING PREFORMATTED TEXT

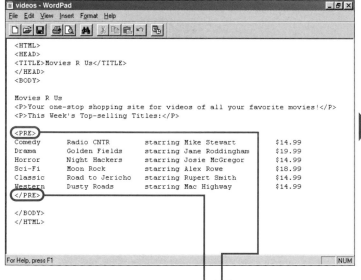

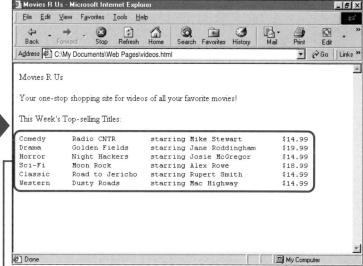

■ Make sure you use spaces, not tabs, to line up columns of information. You should also use a monospaced font, such as Courier, so you can see exactly how the text will appear in a Web browser.

1 Type **<PRE>** in front of the text you want to display as preformatted text.

2 Type **</PRE>** after the text you want to display as preformatted text.

■ The Web browser displays the text with the same spacing you used when creating the Web page.

■ To display your Web page in a Web browser, see pages 32 to 35.

ADD A COMMENT

You can add a comment to your Web page that will not appear when readers view your Web page.

Comment: Add pictures of birds the next time this Web page is updated.

You can add comments to remind you to update a section of text or indicate why you used a specific tag.

ADD A COMMENT

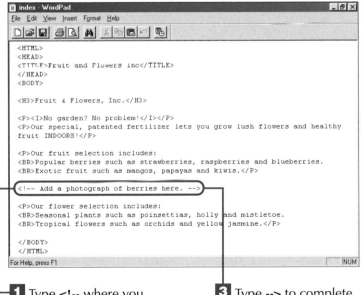

1 Type **<!--** where you want to add a comment. Then press the **Spacebar**.

2 Type the comment. Then press the **Spacebar**.

3 Type **-->** to complete the comment.

■ The Web browser does not display the comment on your Web page.

■ To display your Web page in a Web browser, see pages 32 to 35.

■ Keep in mind that readers can choose to view the HTML tags you used to create your Web page. Readers who view the HTML tags will be able to read any comments you added to the Web page.

You must perform the steps below to add characters that are used for creating Web pages, such as <, >, " or &.

INSERT SPECIAL CHARACTERS

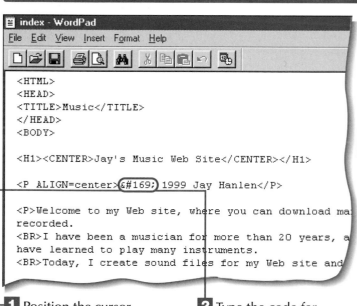

1 Position the cursor where you want the special character to appear on your Web page.

2 Type the code for the special character (example: ©).

■ The Web browser displays the special character.

■ To display your Web page in a Web browser, see pages 32 to 35.

■ The appearance of the special character depends on the Web browser and font settings a reader uses.

SPECIAL CHARACTERS

Character	Code	Character	Code	Character	Code	Character	Code
"	&#34;	¸	&#184;	Ò	&#210;	ì	&#236;
&	&#38;	¹	&#185;	Ó	&#211;	í	&#237;
<	&#60;	º	&#186;	Ô	&#212;	î	&#238;
>	&#62;	»	&#187;	Õ	&#213;	ï	&#239;
¡	&#161;	¼	&#188;	Ö	&#214;	ð	&#240;
¢	&#162;	½	&#189;	×	&#215;	ñ	&#241;
£	&#163;	¾	&#190;	Ø	&#216;	ò	&#242;
¤	&#164;	¿	&#191;	Ù	&#217;	ó	&#243;
¥	&#165;	À	&#192;	Ú	&#218;	ô	&#244;
¦	&#166;	Á	&#193;	Û	&#219;	õ	&#245;
§	&#167;	Â	&#194;	Ü	&#220;	ö	&#246;
¨	&#168;	Ã	&#195;	Ý	&#221;	÷	&#247;
©	&#169;	Ä	&#196;	Þ	&#222;	ø	&#248;
ª	&#170;	Å	&#197;	ß	&#223;	ù	&#249;
«	&#171;	Æ	&#198;	à	&#224;	ú	&#250;
¬	&#172;	Ç	&#199;	á	&#225;	û	&#251;
®	&#174;	È	&#200;	â	&#226;	ü	&#252;
¯	&#175;	É	&#201;	ã	&#227;	ý	&#253;
°	&#176;	Ê	&#202;	ä	&#228;	þ	&#254;
±	&#177;	Ë	&#203;	å	&#229;	ÿ	&#255;
²	&#178;	Ì	&#204;	æ	&#230;		
³	&#179;	Í	&#205;	ç	&#231;		
´	&#180;	Î	&#206;	è	&#232;		
µ	&#181;	Ï	&#207;	é	&#233;		
¶	&#182;	Ð	&#208;	ê	&#234;		
·	&#183;	Ñ	&#209;	ë	&#235;		

CHAPTER 4

CHANGE APPEARANCE OF TEXT

Are you wondering how to change the appearance of text on your Web pages? Read this chapter to learn how.

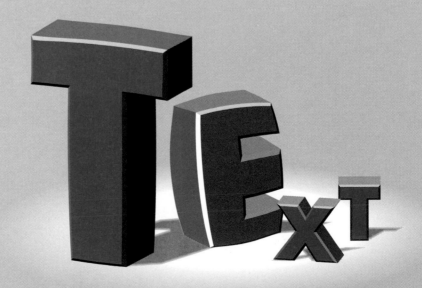

BOLD OR ITALICIZE TEXT

The Guide to Good Gardening

Bold ↗

Italic ↘

By: Roger Greene

You can bold or italicize text to emphasize information on your Web page.

BOLD OR ITALICIZE TEXT

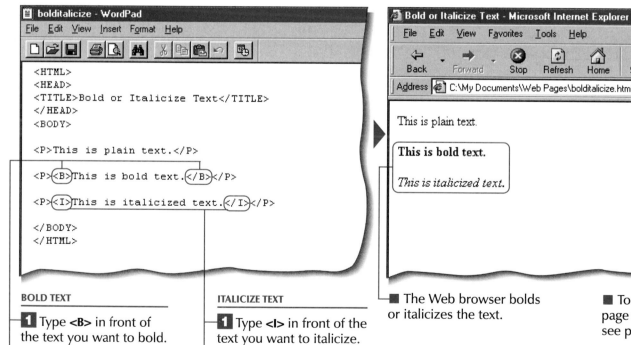

```
<HTML>
<HEAD>
<TITLE>Bold or Italicize Text</TITLE>
</HEAD>
<BODY>

<P>This is plain text.</P>

<P><B>This is bold text.</B></P>

<P><I>This is italicized text.</I></P>

</BODY>
</HTML>
```

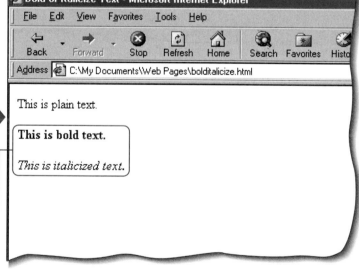

This is plain text.

This is bold text.

This is italicized text.

BOLD TEXT

1 Type **\<B>** in front of the text you want to bold.

2 Type **\</B>** after the text you want to bold.

ITALICIZE TEXT

1 Type **\<I>** in front of the text you want to italicize.

2 Type **\</I>** after the text you want to italicize.

■ The Web browser bolds or italicizes the text.

■ To display your Web page in a Web browser, see pages 32 to 35.

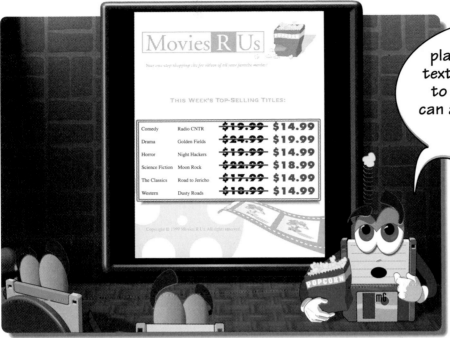

You can place a line through text to show changes to information. You can also underline text to emphasize information.

Companies often strike out old prices to show that new prices are lower.

Be careful when underlining text, since readers may think the text is a link. For information on links, see pages 102 to 113.

STRIKE OUT OR UNDERLINE TEXT

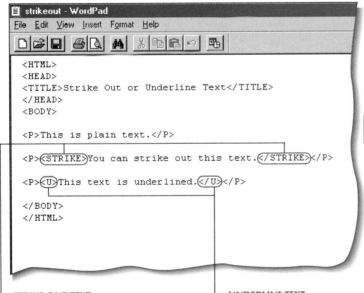

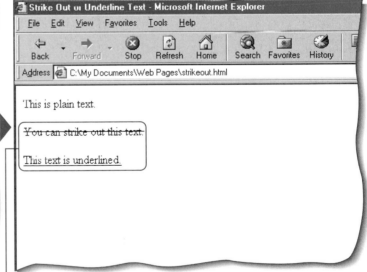

STRIKE OUT TEXT

1 Type **<STRIKE>** in front of the text you want to strike out.

2 Type **</STRIKE>** after the text you want to strike out.

UNDERLINE TEXT

1 Type **<U>** in front of the text you want to underline.

2 Type **</U>** after the text you want to underline.

■ The Web browser displays a line through or under the text.

■ To display your Web page in a Web browser, see pages 32 to 35.

Note: The STRIKE and U tags are still supported by Web browsers, but the use of style sheets is now preferred. For information on style sheets, see page 172.

SUPERSCRIPT OR SUBSCRIPT TEXT

You can place text or numbers slightly above or below the main text on your Web page.

Superscript

$$X^2 * X^3 = 243$$

Subscript

$$X_0 * X_1 - X_2 = 86$$

Superscripts and subscripts are ideal for displaying mathematical equations.

SUPERSCRIPT OR SUBSCRIPT TEXT

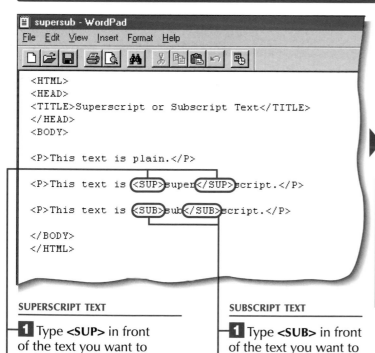

```
<HTML>
<HEAD>
<TITLE>Superscript or Subscript Text</TITLE>
</HEAD>
<BODY>

<P>This text is plain.</P>

<P>This text is <SUP>super</SUP>script.</P>

<P>This text is <SUB>sub</SUB>script.</P>

</BODY>
</HTML>
```

This text is plain.

This text is ^{super}script.

This text is $_{sub}$script.

SUPERSCRIPT TEXT

1 Type **<SUP>** in front of the text you want to superscript.

2 Type **</SUP>** after the text you want to superscript.

SUBSCRIPT TEXT

1 Type **<SUB>** in front of the text you want to subscript.

2 Type **</SUB>** after the text you want to subscript.

■ The Web browser displays the text slightly above or below the main text on your Web page.

■ To display your Web page in a Web browser, see pages 32 to 35.

50

You can make text on your Web page look like it was produced by a typewriter.

Typewriter text is often used to show information a reader can enter into a computer.

USING TYPEWRITER TEXT

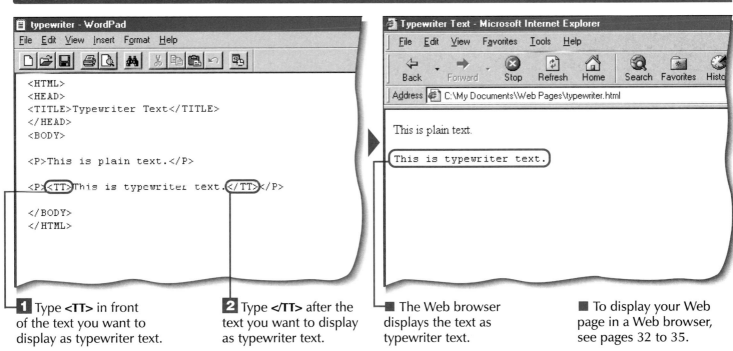

typewriter - WordPad

File   Edit   View   Insert   Format   Help

```
<HTML>
<HEAD>
<TITLE>Typewriter Text</TITLE>
</HEAD>
<BODY>

<P>This is plain text.</P>

<P><TT>This is typewriter text.</TT></P>

</BODY>
</HTML>
```

Typewriter Text - Microsoft Internet Explorer

File   Edit   View   Favorites   Tools   Help

Back   Forward   Stop   Refresh   Home   Search   Favorites   Histo

Address   C:\My Documents\Web Pages\typewriter.html

This is plain text.

This is typewriter text.

1 Type **<TT>** in front of the text you want to display as typewriter text.

2 Type **</TT>** after the text you want to display as typewriter text.

■ The Web browser displays the text as typewriter text.

■ To display your Web page in a Web browser, see pages 32 to 35.

Ludwig van Beethoven was born in Bonn, Germany in 1770. He spent most of his life giving concerts, teaching piano and selling his compositions.

Beethoven

in Bonn,
t of his life
nd selling

Bach

Johann Sebastian _was born into a_
of musicians _in Eisenach, Germany_
Bach's w_clude church organ and cho_
music_ or chamber orchestras and_
200 cantatas.

Brush Script MT

You can change the font of a section of text to customize the appearance of your Web page.

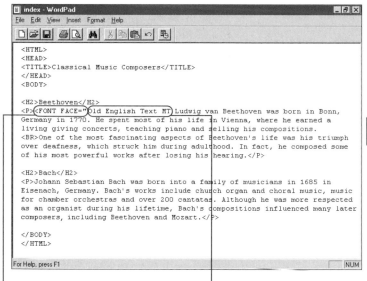

```
index - WordPad
File  Edit  View  Insert  Format  Help

<HTML>
<HEAD>
<TITLE>Classical Music Composers</TITLE>
</HEAD>
<BODY>

<H2>Beethoven</H2>
<P><FONT FACE="Old English Text MT>Ludwig van Beethoven was born in Bonn,
Germany in 1770. He spent most of his life in Vienna, where he earned a
living giving concerts, teaching piano and selling his compositions.
<BR>One of the most fascinating aspects of Beethoven's life was his triumph
over deafness, which struck him during adulthood. In fact, he composed some
of his most powerful works after losing his hearing.</P>

<H2>Bach</H2>
<P>Johann Sebastian Bach was born into a family of musicians in 1685 in
Eisenach, Germany. Bach's works include church organ and choral music, music
for chamber orchestras and over 200 cantatas. Although he was more respected
as an organist during his lifetime, Bach's compositions influenced many later
composers, including Beethoven and Mozart.</P>

</BODY>
</HTML>

For Help, press F1                                          NUM
```

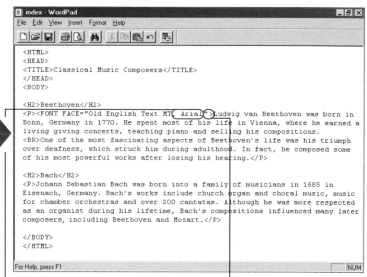

```
index - WordPad
File  Edit  View  Insert  Format  Help

<HTML>
<HEAD>
<TITLE>Classical Music Composers</TITLE>
</HEAD>
<BODY>

<H2>Beethoven</H2>
<P><FONT FACE="Old English Text MT, Arial">Ludwig van Beethoven was born in
Bonn, Germany in 1770. He spent most of his life in Vienna, where he earned a
living giving concerts, teaching piano and selling his compositions.
<BR>One of the most fascinating aspects of Beethoven's life was his triumph
over deafness, which struck him during adulthood. In fact, he composed some
of his most powerful works after losing his hearing.</P>

<H2>Bach</H2>
<P>Johann Sebastian Bach was born into a family of musicians in 1685 in
Eisenach, Germany. Bach's works include church organ and choral music, music
for chamber orchestras and over 200 cantatas. Although he was more respected
as an organist during his lifetime, Bach's compositions influenced many later
composers, including Beethoven and Mozart.</P>

</BODY>
</HTML>

For Help, press F1                                          NUM
```

1 Type **<FONT FACE="** in front of the text you want to change.

2 Type the name of the font you want to use.

■ Instead of typing the name of a font, you can specify a font type (**serif**, **sans-serif** or **monospace**).

3 To specify a second font choice, type a comma (**,**) and then press the **Spacebar**. Then type your second font choice.

Note: For information on specifying more than one font, see the top of page 53.

4 Type **">** to complete the FONT tag.

TIP

Why should I specify more than one font?

You should specify more than one font in case your first font choice is not available on a reader's computer. One of the fonts you specify should be a common font, such as Arial, to increase the probability that your Web page will display one of your font choices.

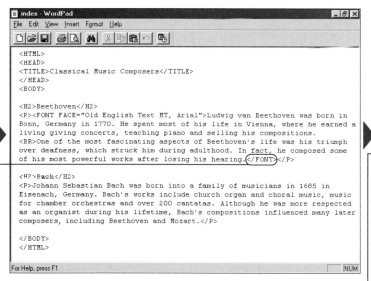

5 Type **</FONT>** after the text you want to change.

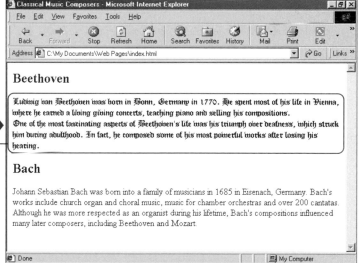

■ The Web browser displays the text in the font you specified.

■ To display your Web page in a Web browser, see pages 32 to 35.

Note: The FONT tag is still supported by Web browsers, but the use of style sheets is now preferred. For information on style sheets, see page 172.

CHANGE FONT SIZE

You can change the size of text on all or part of your Web page.

Larger text is easier to read, but smaller text allows you to fit more information on a screen.

CHANGE ALL TEXT

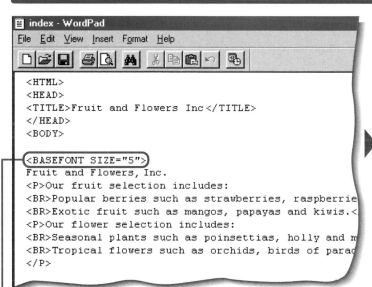

```
<HTML>
<HEAD>
<TITLE>Fruit and Flowers Inc</TITLE>
</HEAD>
<BODY>

<BASEFONT SIZE="5">
Fruit and Flowers, Inc.
<P>Our fruit selection includes:
<BR>Popular berries such as strawberries, raspberrie
<BR>Exotic fruit such as mangos, papayas and kiwis.<
<P>Our flower selection includes:
<BR>Seasonal plants such as poinsettias, holly and m
<BR>Tropical flowers such as orchids, birds of para
</P>
```

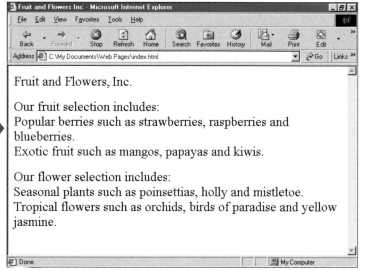

Fruit and Flowers, Inc.

Our fruit selection includes:
Popular berries such as strawberries, raspberries and blueberries.
Exotic fruit such as mangos, papayas and kiwis.

Our flower selection includes:
Seasonal plants such as poinsettias, holly and mistletoe.
Tropical flowers such as orchids, birds of paradise and yellow jasmine.

1 Type **<BASEFONT SIZE="?">** before the text on your Web page. Replace **?** with a number from 1 to 7. The smallest font size is 1; the largest font size is 7.

■ The Web browser displays the text at the new size.

■ To display your Web page in a Web browser, see pages 32 to 35.

■ The BASEFONT tag will not affect the size of headings on your Web page. For information on headings, see page 40.

Note: The BASEFONT tag is still supported by Web browsers, but the use of style sheets is now preferred. For information on style sheets, see page 172.

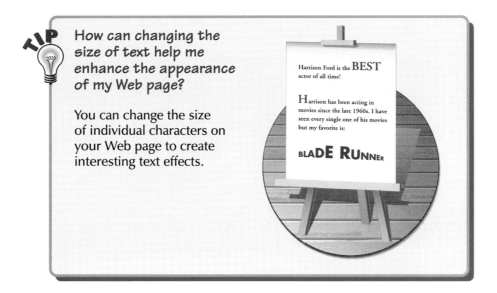

TIP

How can changing the size of text help me enhance the appearance of my Web page?

You can change the size of individual characters on your Web page to create interesting text effects.

CHANGE SECTION OF TEXT

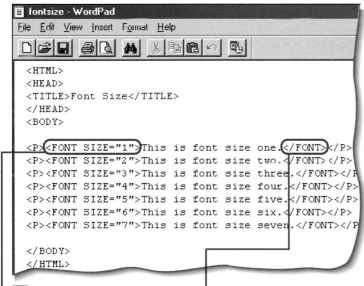

```
<HTML>
<HEAD>
<TITLE>Font Size</TITLE>
</HEAD>
<BODY>

<P><FONT SIZE="1">This is font size one.</FONT></P>
<P><FONT SIZE="2">This is font size two.</FONT> </P>
<P> <FONT SIZE="3">This is font size three.</FONT></P>
<P><FONT SIZE="4">This is font size four.</FONT></P>
<P><FONT SIZE="5">This is font size five.</FONT></P>
<P><FONT SIZE="6">This is font size six.</FONT></P>
<P><FONT SIZE="7">This is font size seven.</FONT></P>

</BODY>
</HTML>
```

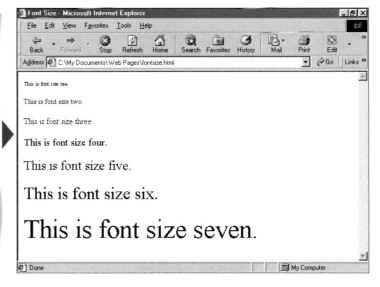

1 Type **<FONT SIZE="?">** in front of the text you want to change. Replace **?** with a number from 1 to 7. The smallest font size is 1; the largest font size is 7.

Note: You can type a plus (+) or minus (-) sign before the number to specify a size relative to the surrounding text. For example, type +2 to make the text two sizes larger than the surrounding text.

2 Type **</FONT>** after the text you want to change.

■ The Web browser displays the text at the new size.

■ To display your Web page in a Web browser, see pages 32 to 35.

Note: The FONT tag is still supported by Web browsers, but the use of style sheets is now preferred. For information on style sheets, see page 172.

You can change the color of text on all or part of your Web page.

The colors you choose for your Web page may not appear the way you expect on some computers. Readers can set their Web browsers to override the colors you choose.

CHANGE ALL TEXT

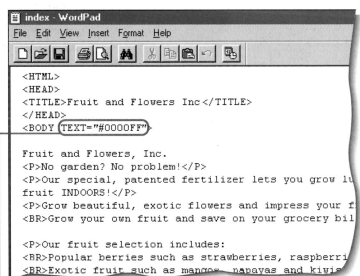

```
<HTML>
<HEAD>
<TITLE>Fruit and Flowers Inc</TITLE>
</HEAD>
<BODY TEXT="#0000FF">

Fruit and Flowers, Inc.
<P>No garden? No problem!</P>
<P>Our special, patented fertilizer lets you grow lu
fruit INDOORS!</P>
<P>Grow beautiful, exotic flowers and impress your f:
<BR>Grow your own fruit and save on your grocery bil

<P>Our fruit selection includes:
<BR>Popular berries such as strawberries, raspberri
<BR>Exotic fruit such as mangos, papayas and kiwi
```

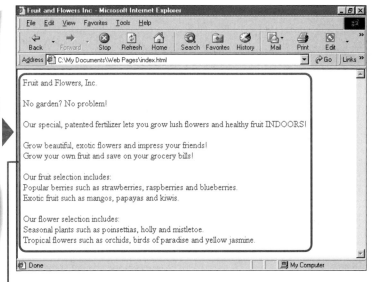

1 In the <BODY> tag, type **TEXT="?"** replacing **?** with the name or code for the color you want to use (example: blue or #0000FF).

Note: For a list of colors, see the top of page 57.

■ The Web browser displays all the text on the Web page in the color you selected.

■ To display your Web page in a Web browser, see pages 32 to 35.

Note: The TEXT attribute is still supported by Web browsers, but the use of style sheets is now preferred. For information on style sheets, see page 172.

What colors can I use on my Web pages?

Here are some colors commonly used on Web pages. There are only 16 colors you can specify by name. You can find a more complete list of colors at the front of this book.

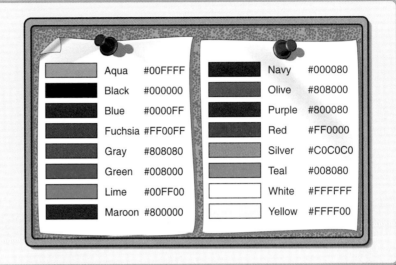

Aqua	#00FFFF	
Black	#000000	
Blue	#0000FF	
Fuchsia	#FF00FF	
Gray	#808080	
Green	#008000	
Lime	#00FF00	
Maroon	#800000	
Navy	#000080	
Olive	#808000	
Purple	#800080	
Red	#FF0000	
Silver	#C0C0C0	
Teal	#008080	
White	#FFFFFF	
Yellow	#FFFF00	

CHANGE SECTION OF TEXT

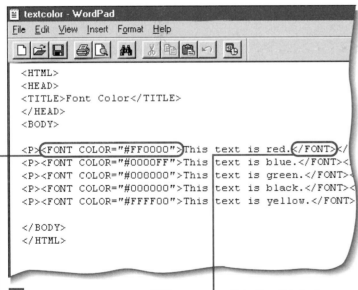

```
<HTML>
<HEAD>
<TITLE>Font Color</TITLE>
</HEAD>
<BODY>

<P><FONT COLOR="#FF0000">This text is red.</FONT></
<P><FONT COLOR="#0000FF">This text is blue.</FONT><
<P><FONT COLOR="#000000">This text is green.</FONT>
<P><FONT COLOR="#000000">This text is black.</FONT><
<P><FONT COLOR="#FFFF00">This text is yellow.</FONT>

</BODY>
</HTML>
```

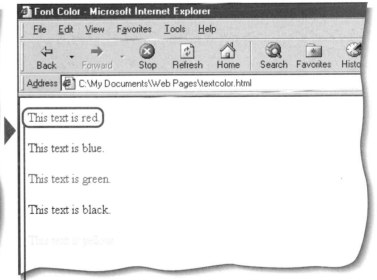

1 Type **<FONT COLOR="?">** in front of the text you want to change. Replace **?** with the name or code for the color you want to use (example: red or #FF0000).

Note: For a list of colors, see the top of this page.

2 Type **</FONT>** after the text you want to change.

■ The Web browser displays the text in the color you selected.

■ To display your Web page in a Web browser, see pages 32 to 35.

Note: The FONT tag is still supported by Web browsers, but the use of style sheets is now preferred. For information on style sheets, see page 172.

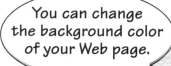

You can change the background color of your Web page.

Make sure you select a background color that works well with the color of your text. For example, red text on a blue background can be difficult to read.

CHANGE BACKGROUND COLOR

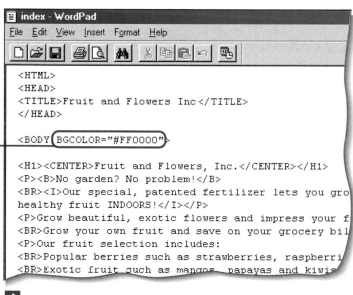

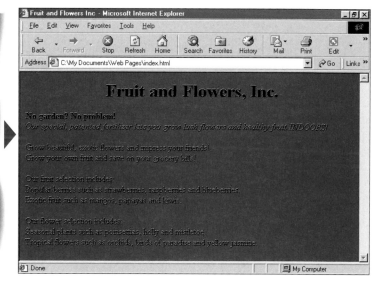

1 In the <BODY> tag, type **BGCOLOR="?"** replacing **?** with the name or code for the color you want to use (example: red or #FF0000).

Note: For a list of colors, see the top of page 57.

■ The Web browser displays the background color you selected.

■ To display your Web page in a Web browser, see pages 32 to 35.

Note: The BGCOLOR attribute is still supported by Web browsers, but the use of style sheets is now preferred. For information on style sheets, see page 172.

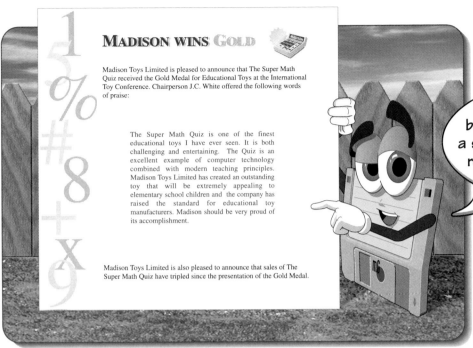

MADISON WINS GOLD

Madison Toys Limited is pleased to announce that The Super Math Quiz received the Gold Medal for Educational Toys at the International Toy Conference. Chairperson J.C. White offered the following words of praise:

> The Super Math Quiz is one of the finest educational toys I have ever seen. It is both challenging and entertaining. The Quiz is an excellent example of computer technology combined with modern teaching principles. Madison Toys Limited has created an outstanding toy that will be extremely appealing to elementary school children and the company has raised the standard for educational toy manufacturers. Madison should be very proud of its accomplishment.

Madison Toys Limited is also pleased to announce that sales of The Super Math Quiz have tripled since the presentation of the Gold Medal.

You can create a block quote to separate a section of text from the rest of the text on your Web page.

Block quotes are often used for displaying long quotations.

CREATE A BLOCK QUOTE

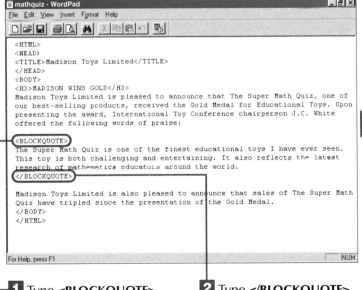

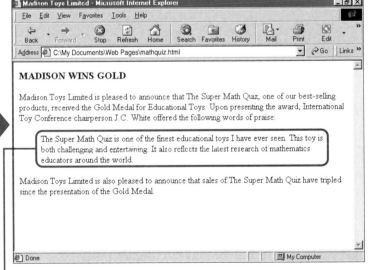

1 Type **<BLOCKQUOTE>** before the text you want to display as a block quote.

2 Type **</BLOCKQUOTE>** after the text you want to display as a block quote.

■ The Web browser displays the text as a block quote. Block quotes are usually indented from both sides of the Web page.

■ To display your Web page in a Web browser, see pages 32 to 35.

CREATE AN ORDERED LIST

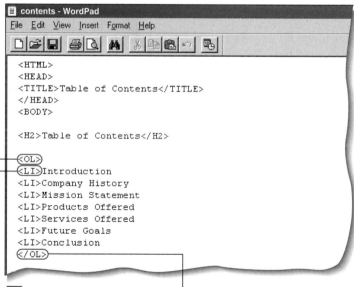

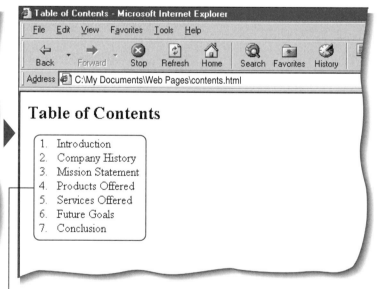

1 Type **<OL>** before the list.

2 Type **<LI>** in front of each item in the list.

■ If you want to continue an item in the list on the next line without creating a new list item, use the BR tag. For information on the BR tag, see page 38.

3 Type **</OL>** after the list.

■ The Web browser displays the ordered list. A number appears in front of each item in the list.

■ To display your Web page in a Web browser, see pages 32 to 35.

Note: You can add a new item to the ordered list at any time. The Web browser will automatically renumber the items in the list.

What number styles can I use for my ordered list?

You can use one of the following number styles for your ordered list.

NUMBER STYLE	RESULT
A	A,B,C
a	a,b,c
I	I,II,III
i	i,ii,iii
1	1,2,3

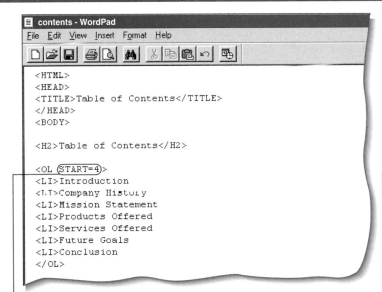

```
<HTML>
<HEAD>
<TITLE>Table of Contents</TITLE>
</HEAD>
<BODY>

<H2>Table of Contents</H2>

<OL START=4>
<LI>Introduction
<LI>Company History
<LI>Mission Statement
<LI>Products Offered
<LI>Services Offered
<LI>Future Goals
<LI>Conclusion
</OL>
```

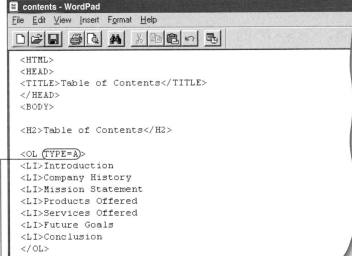

```
<HTML>
<HEAD>
<TITLE>Table of Contents</TITLE>
</HEAD>
<BODY>

<H2>Table of Contents</H2>

<OL TYPE=A>
<LI>Introduction
<LI>Company History
<LI>Mission Statement
<LI>Products Offered
<LI>Services Offered
<LI>Future Goals
<LI>Conclusion
</OL>
```

CHANGE STARTING NUMBER

Ordered lists automatically start with the number 1. You can start a list with a different number.

1 In the <OL> tag, type **START=?** replacing **?** with the number you want to use to start the list.

Note: The START attribute is still supported by Web browsers, but the use of style sheets is now preferred. For information on style sheets, see page 172.

CHANGE NUMBER STYLE

You can change the number style of an ordered list.

1 In the <OL> tag, type **TYPE=?** replacing **?** with the number style you want to use. For a list of number styles, see the top of this page.

Note: The TYPE attribute is still supported by Web browsers, but the use of style sheets is now preferred. For information on style sheets, see page 172.

You can create an unordered list to display items that are in no particular order, such as a list of products or Web sites.

Our Most Popular Types of Pasta:

- Cannelloni
- Lasagna
- Linguine
- Manicotti
- Ravioli
- Spaghetti

CREATE AN UNORDERED LIST

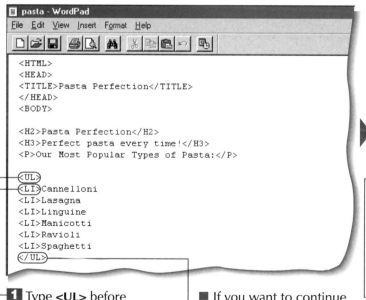

```
<HTML>
<HEAD>
<TITLE>Pasta Perfection</TITLE>
</HEAD>
<BODY>

<H2>Pasta Perfection</H2>
<H3>Perfect pasta every time!</H3>
<P>Our Most Popular Types of Pasta:</P>

<UL>
<LI>Cannelloni
<LI>Lasagna
<LI>Linguine
<LI>Manicotti
<LI>Ravioli
<LI>Spaghetti
</UL>
```

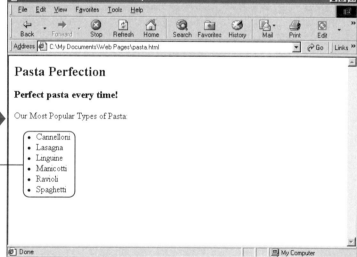

1 Type **<UL>** before the list.

2 Type **<LI>** in front of each item in the list.

■ If you want to continue an item in the list on the next line without creating a new list item, use the BR tag. For information on the BR tag, see page 38.

3 Type **</UL>** after the list.

■ The Web browser displays the unordered list. A bullet (•) appears in front of each item in the list.

■ To display your Web page in a Web browser, see pages 32 to 35.

CREATE A DEFINITION LIST

You can create a definition list to display terms and their definitions. This type of list is ideal for a glossary.

CREATE A DEFINITION LIST

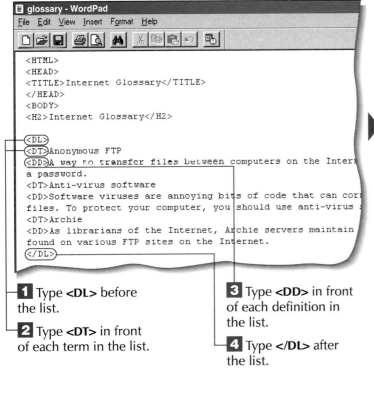

```
<HTML>
<HEAD>
<TITLE>Internet Glossary</TITLE>
</HEAD>
<BODY>
<H2>Internet Glossary</H2>

<DL>
<DT>Anonymous FTP
<DD>A way to transfer files between computers on the Interr
a password.
<DT>Anti-virus software
<DD>Software viruses are annoying bits of code that can corr
files. To protect your computer, you should use anti-virus :
<DT>Archie
<DD>As librarians of the Internet, Archie servers maintain
found on various FTP sites on the Internet.
</DL>
```

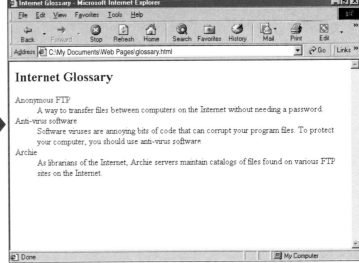

1 Type **<DL>** before the list.

2 Type **<DT>** in front of each term in the list.

3 Type **<DD>** in front of each definition in the list.

4 Type **</DL>** after the list.

■ The Web browser displays the definition list. Each definition is indented from the left side of the Web page.

■ To display your Web page in a Web browser, see pages 32 to 35.

BIRD WATCHERS' HOME PAGE

The page dedicated to people who love to watch birds!

Bird watchers appreciate the beauty and wonder of birds, and this month, with summer just around the corner, we will discuss the best spots for birdwatching in the national parks of the northern states. These locations have all been recommended by visitors to our page. If you have a new location to add, please email us today!

Popular Nesting Sites

Nests

Bird in Flight

CHAPTER 5

ADD IMAGES

Would you like to add images to your Web pages? Find out how in this chapter.

Background Images

INTRODUCTION TO IMAGES

REASONS FOR USING IMAGES

ART

A Web page can display drawings, paintings or computer-generated art. Many people display their favorite paintings or their children's artwork. Graphic artists and design companies often display art on their Web pages to advertise their work.

ILLUSTRATIONS

An image can help illustrate a concept that is difficult to explain with words. You can include a map to give directions, a chart to show financial trends or a diagram to point out essential parts of a product.

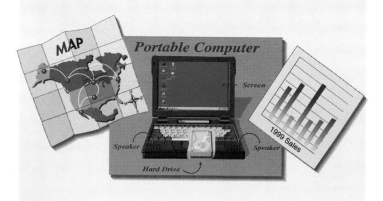

PHOTOGRAPHS

You can display photographs of your family, pets or favorite celebrities on your Web pages. Many companies include photographs of their products so people around the world can view the products without having to visit a store or wait for a brochure to arrive in the mail.

NAVIGATIONAL TOOLS

You can use images as navigational tools to help readers browse through your Web pages.

Readers can select the images to move through your Web pages.

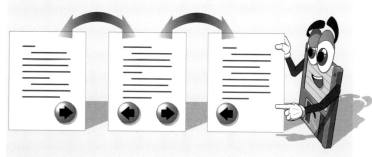

OBTAIN IMAGES

INTERNET

There are many Web sites that offer images you can use for free on your Web pages. Make sure you have permission to use any images you obtain on the Internet. You can find images at the following Web sites:

www.bestclipart.com/photographs/photoframes.htm

www.shannanigan.com/clipart.html

www.noeticart.com

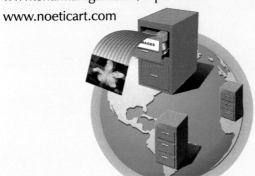

SCAN IMAGES

You can use a scanner to scan images into a computer. You can scan photographs, logos and drawings and then place the scanned images on your Web pages. If you do not have a scanner, many service bureaus will scan images for a fee.

CREATE IMAGES

You can use an image editing program to create your own images. Creating your own images lets you design images that best suit your Web pages. Popular image editing programs include Adobe Photoshop and Paint Shop Pro.

IMAGE COLLECTIONS

You can buy a collection of ready-made images at computer stores. You can obtain image collections that include cartoons, drawings, photographs or computer-generated art. Make sure images you buy are in a format that Web browsers can display, such as GIF or JPEG.

IMAGE CONSIDERATIONS

You should consider several factors when adding images to a Web page.

COPYRIGHT

You may find images in books, newspapers, magazines or on the Internet that you want to add to your Web pages. Make sure you have permission before using any of these images on your Web pages.

IMAGE RESOLUTION

The resolution of an image refers to the clarity of the image. Higher resolution images are sharper and more detailed. Most computer monitors display images at a resolution of 72 dots per inch (dpi).

Images you add to your Web pages do not need resolutions higher than 72 dpi unless you want readers to print the images. Higher resolution images take longer to transfer to a computer.

IMAGE WIDTH

Make sure the images you add to your Web pages are less than 620 pixels wide. An image wider than 620 pixels may not fit on some computer screens. You can use an image editing program to determine the width of an image. For more information, see page 90.

LARGE IMAGES

Large images can increase the time it takes for a Web page to appear on a screen. If you want to include a large image on a Web page, consider creating a thumbnail image. A thumbnail image is a small version of an image that readers can select to display the larger image. This lets readers decide if they want to wait to view the larger image. To create a smaller version of an image, see page 92.

VIEW WEB PAGES WITHOUT IMAGES

Make sure your Web pages will make sense and look attractive if the images are not displayed. Some readers turn off the display of images to browse the Web more quickly, while others use Web browsers that cannot display images.

You can provide alternative text that describes your images for readers who do not see the images. To provide alternative text, see page 74.

REUSE IMAGES

You can use the same image several times on a Web page without increasing the time it takes for the Web page to transfer to a computer. When the same image appears more than once on a Web page, the image transfers only once to a computer. The computer temporarily stores a copy of the image and displays the copy each time the image appears on the Web page.

ADD AN IMAGE

You can add an image to a Web page. An image that appears on a Web page is called an inline image.

For information on where you can find images for your Web pages, see page 67.

ADD AN IMAGE

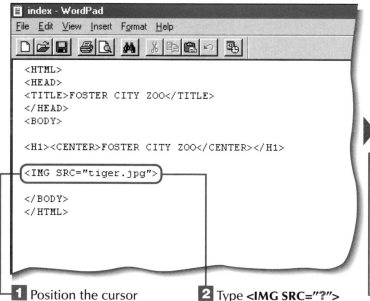

```
<HTML>
<HEAD>
<TITLE>FOSTER CITY ZOO</TITLE>
</HEAD>
<BODY>

<H1><CENTER>FOSTER CITY ZOO</CENTER></H1>

<IMG SRC="tiger.jpg">

</BODY>
</HTML>
```

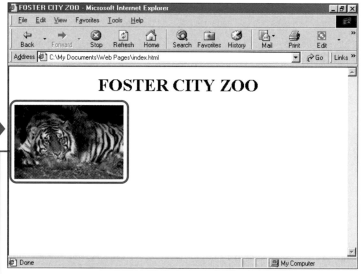

1 Position the cursor where you want the image to appear on your Web page.

2 Type **<IMG SRC="?">** replacing **?** with the location of the image on your computer.

Note: For information on specifying the location of an image, see page 71.

■ The Web browser displays the image on your Web page.

■ To display your Web page in a Web browser, see pages 32 to 35.

TIPS FOR ADDING IMAGES

IMAGE TYPES

When adding images to your Web pages, you should use GIF or JPEG images. GIF and JPEG images are the most popular types of images on the Web. You can use an image editing program to convert an image to the GIF or JPEG format. For more information, see page 88.

IMAGE SIZE

Images increase the time it takes for a Web page to appear on a screen. If a Web page takes too long to appear, readers may lose interest and move to another page. Whenever possible, you should use images with small file sizes since these images will transfer faster.

SPECIFY LOCATION OF IMAGES

You should store all of your Web pages and images in one folder on your computer. If the folder contains many files, you may want to store your images in a subfolder.

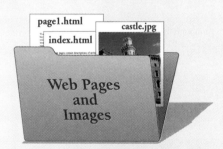

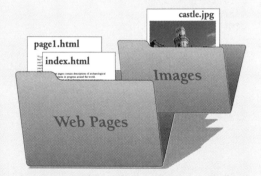

If an image you want to add to a Web page is stored in the same folder as the Web page, you can specify just the name of the image (example: castle.jpg).

If an image is stored in a subfolder, you must specify the name of the subfolder and the name of the image (example: images/castle.jpg).

CENTER AN IMAGE

You can center an image on your Web page to enhance the appearance of the Web page.

CENTER AN IMAGE

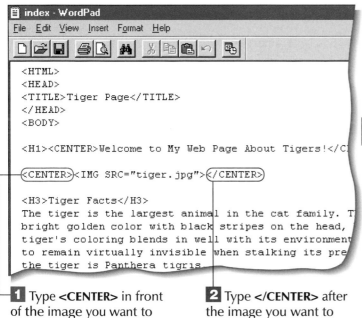

```
<HTML>
<HEAD>
<TITLE>Tiger Page</TITLE>
</HEAD>
<BODY>

<H1><CENTER>Welcome to My Web Page About Tigers!</C

<CENTER><IMG SRC="tiger.jpg"></CENTER>

<H3>Tiger Facts</H3>
The tiger is the largest animal in the cat family. T
bright golden color with black stripes on the head,
tiger's coloring blends in well with its environment
to remain virtually invisible when stalking its pre
the tiger is Panthera tigris
```

1 Type **<CENTER>** in front of the image you want to center.

2 Type **</CENTER>** after the image you want to center.

■ The Web browser centers the image.

■ To display your Web page in a Web browser, see pages 32 to 35.

Note: The CENTER tag is still supported by Web browsers, but the use of style sheets is now preferred. For information on style sheets, see page 172.

ADD A BORDER

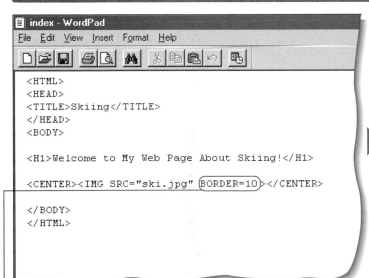

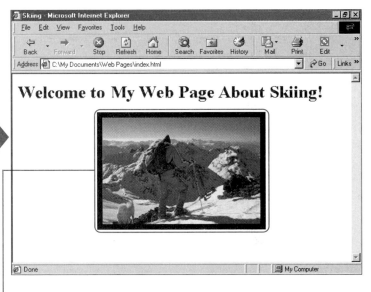

1 In the <IMG> tag for the image you want to display a border, type **BORDER=?** replacing **?** with the border thickness you want to use in pixels.

Note: To remove an existing border, replace ? with the number 0.

■ The Web browser displays a border around the image.

■ To display your Web page in a Web browser, see pages 32 to 35.

Note: The BORDER attribute is still supported by Web browsers, but the use of style sheets is now preferred. For information on style sheets, see page 172.

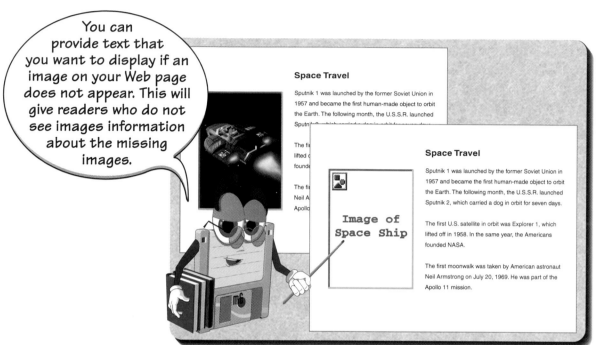

You can provide text that you want to display if an image on your Web page does not appear. This will give readers who do not see images information about the missing images.

Some readers use Web browsers that cannot display images, while others turn off the display of images to browse the Web more quickly.

PROVIDE ALTERNATIVE TEXT

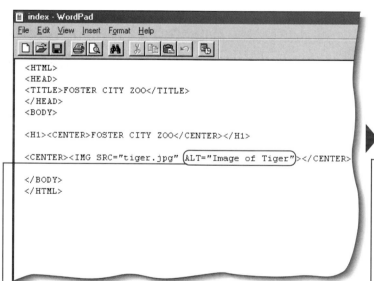

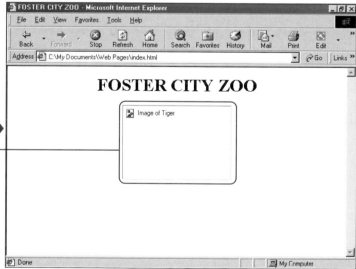

1 In the <IMG> tag for the image you want to offer alternative text, type **ALT="?"** replacing **?** with the text you want to display if the image does not appear.

■ If the image does not appear, the Web browser will display the text you specified.

■ To display your Web page in a Web browser, see pages 32 to 35.

There are three ways you can align an image with text.

If you have wrapped text around an image, you cannot align the image with text. For information on wrapping text around an image, see page 76.

ALIGN AN IMAGE WITH TEXT

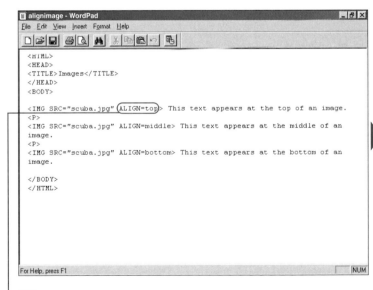

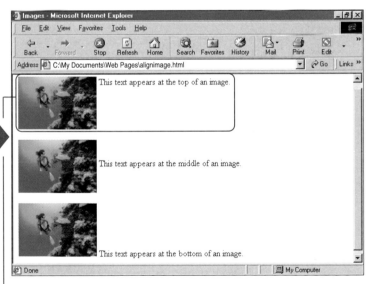

1 In the <IMG> tag for the image you want to align with text, type **ALIGN=?** replacing **?** with the way you want to align the image with the text (**top**, **bottom** or **middle**).

■ The Web browser aligns the image with the text.

■ To display your Web page in a Web browser, see pages 32 to 35.

Note: The ALIGN attribute is still supported by Web browsers, but the use of style sheets is now preferred. For information on style sheets, see page 172.

WRAP TEXT AROUND AN IMAGE

You can wrap text around an image to give your Web page a professional look.

If you have aligned an image with text, you cannot wrap text around the image. For information on aligning an image with text, see page 75.

WRAP TEXT AROUND AN IMAGE

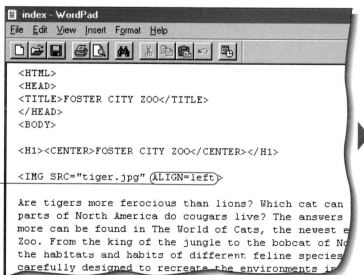

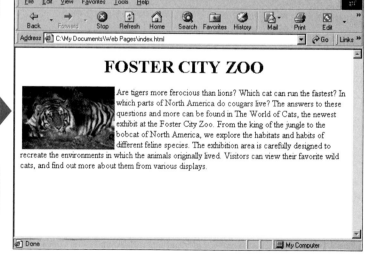

1 To wrap text around the right side of an image, type **ALIGN=left** in the <IMG> tag for the image.

■ To wrap text around the left side of an image, type **ALIGN=right** in the <IMG> tag for the image.

■ The Web browser displays the text wrapped around the image.

■ To display your Web page in a Web browser, see pages 32 to 35.

Note: The ALIGN attribute is still supported by Web browsers, but the use of style sheets is now preferred. For information on style sheets, see page 172.

You can stop text from wrapping around an image. You can have the text continue when the left, right or both margins are clear of images.

STOP TEXT WRAP

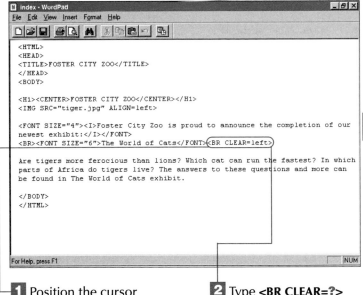

```
<HTML>
<HEAD>
<TITLE>FOSTER CITY ZOO</TITLE>
</HEAD>
<BODY>

<H1><CENTER>FOSTER CITY ZOO</CENTER></H1>
<IMG SRC="tiger.jpg" ALIGN=left>

<FONT SIZE="4"><I>Foster City Zoo is proud to announce the completion of our
newest exhibit:</I></FONT>
<BR><FONT SIZE="6">The World of Cats</FONT><BR CLEAR=left>

Are tigers more ferocious than lions? Which cat can run the fastest? In which
parts of Africa do tigers live? The answers to these questions and more can
be found in The World of Cats exhibit.

</BODY>
</HTML>
```

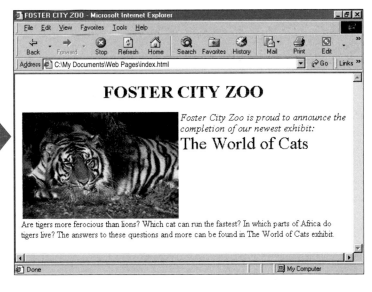

1 Position the cursor where you want to stop text from wrapping around an image.

2 Type **<BR CLEAR=?>** replacing **?** with the margin(s) you want to be clear of images before the text continues (**left**, **right** or **all**).

■ The Web browser stops the text wrap where you specified.

■ To display your Web page in a Web browser, see pages 32 to 35.

Note: The CLEAR attribute is still supported by Web browsers, but the use of style sheets is now preferred. For information on style sheets, see page 172.

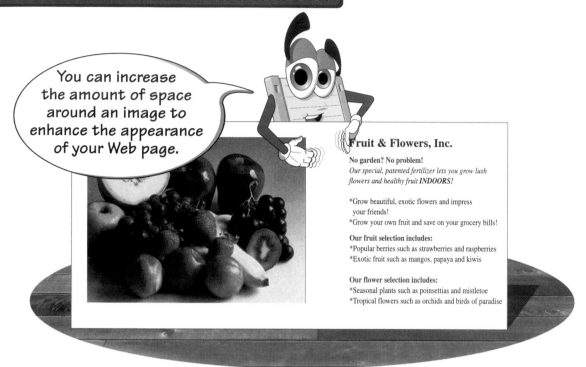

You can increase the amount of space around an image to enhance the appearance of your Web page.

Fruit & Flowers, Inc.

No garden? No problem!
Our special, patented fertilizer lets you grow lush flowers and healthy fruit INDOORS!

*Grow beautiful, exotic flowers and impress
 your friends!
*Grow your own fruit and save on your grocery bills!

Our fruit selection includes:
*Popular berries such as strawberries and raspberries
*Exotic fruit such as mangos, papaya and kiwis

Our flower selection includes:
*Seasonal plants such as poinsettias and mistletoe
*Tropical flowers such as orchids and birds of paradise

ADD SPACE AROUND AN IMAGE

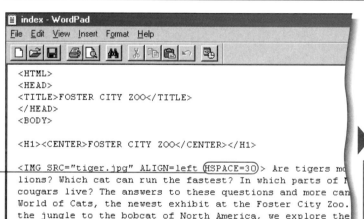

LEFT AND RIGHT SIDES

1 In the <IMG> tag for the image you want to add space around, type **HSPACE=?** replacing **?** with the amount of space you want to add to both the left and right sides of the image in pixels.

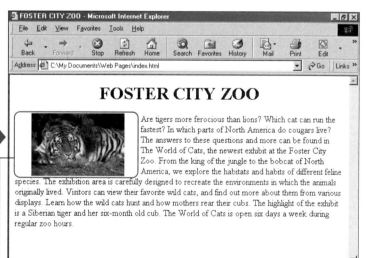

■ The Web browser adds space to the left and right sides of the image.

■ To display your Web page in a Web browser, see pages 32 to 35.

Note: The HSPACE attribute is still supported by Web browsers, but the use of style sheets is now preferred. For information on style sheets, see page 172.

Why should I increase the amount of space around an image?

Increasing the amount of space between an image and the surrounding text will make the text easier to read.

Increasing the amount of space between two images that appear side by side will prevent the images from appearing as one large image.

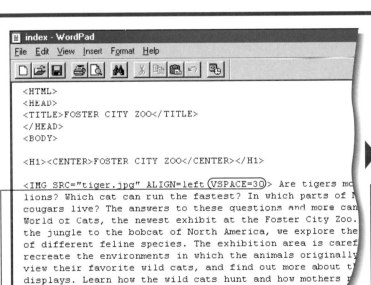

```
<HTML>
<HEAD>
<TITLE>FOSTER CITY ZOO</TITLE>
</HEAD>
<BODY>

<H1><CENTER>FOSTER CITY ZOO</CENTER></H1>

<IMG SRC="tiger.jpg" ALIGN=left VSPACE=30> Are tigers mc
lions? Which cat can run the fastest? In which parts of N
cougars live? The answers to these questions and more can
World of Cats, the newest exhibit at the Foster City Zoo.
the jungle to the bobcat of North America, we explore the
of different feline species. The exhibition area is caref
recreate the environments in which the animals originally
view their favorite wild cats, and find out more about t
displays. Learn how the wild cats hunt and how mothers r
highlight of the exhibit is a Siberian tiger and her s
```

TOP AND BOTTOM

1 In the <IMG> tag for the image you want to add space around, type **VSPACE=?** replacing **?** with the amount of space you want to add to both the top and bottom of the image in pixels.

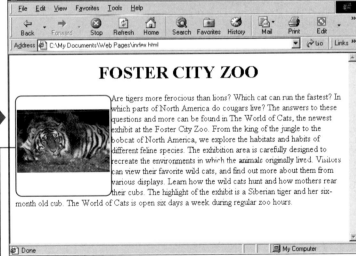

FOSTER CITY ZOO

Are tigers more ferocious than lions? Which cat can run the fastest? In which parts of North America do cougars live? The answers to these questions and more can be found in The World of Cats, the newest exhibit at the Foster City Zoo. From the king of the jungle to the bobcat of North America, we explore the habitats and habits of different feline species. The exhibition area is carefully designed to recreate the environments in which the animals originally lived. Visitors can view their favorite wild cats, and find out more about them from various displays. Learn how the wild cats hunt and how mothers rear their cubs. The highlight of the exhibit is a Siberian tiger and her six-month old cub. The World of Cats is open six days a week during regular zoo hours.

■ The Web browser adds space to the top and bottom of the image.

■ To display your Web page in a Web browser, see pages 32 to 35.

Note: The VSPACE attribute is still supported by Web browsers, but the use of style sheets is now preferred. For information on style sheets, see page 172.

ADD A BACKGROUND IMAGE

You can have a small image repeat to fill an entire Web page. This can add an interesting background design to your Web page.

ADD A BACKGROUND IMAGE

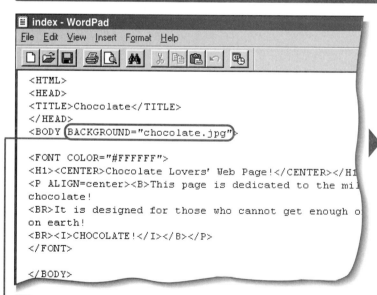

```
index - WordPad
File  Edit  View  Insert  Format  Help

<HTML>
<HEAD>
<TITLE>Chocolate</TITLE>
</HEAD>
<BODY BACKGROUND="chocolate.jpg">

<FONT COLOR="#FFFFFF">
<H1><CENTER>Chocolate Lovers' Web Page!</CENTER></H1
<P ALIGN=center><B>This page is dedicated to the mil
chocolate!
<BR>It is designed for those who cannot get enough o
on earth!
<BR><I>CHOCOLATE!</I></B></P>
</FONT>

</BODY>
```

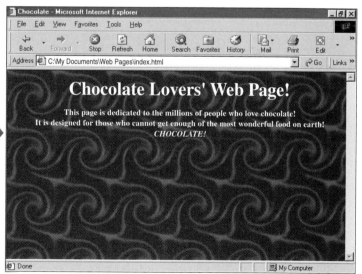

1 In the <BODY> tag, type **BACKGROUND="?"** replacing **?** with the location of the image on your computer.

Note: For information on specifying the location of an image, see page 71.

■ The Web browser repeats the image to fill the entire Web page.

■ To display your Web page in a Web browser, see pages 32 to 35.

Note: The BACKGROUND attribute is still supported by Web browsers, but the use of style sheets is now preferred. For information on style sheets, see page 172.

TIPS FOR ADDING BACKGROUND IMAGES

CHOOSE A BACKGROUND IMAGE

Choose an image that creates an interesting background design without overwhelming your Web page. Since background images increase the time it takes for a Web page to appear on a screen, you should choose a background image with a small file size.

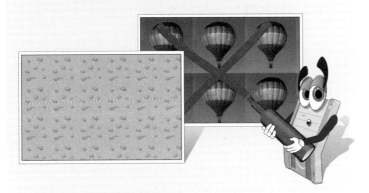

SEAMLESS BACKGROUND

A good background image should have invisible edges. When the image repeats to fill the Web page, you should not be able to tell where the edges of the images meet.

WEB PAGE READABILITY

Make sure the background image you choose does not affect the readability of your Web page. You may need to change the color of text to make the Web page easier to read. To change the color of text, see page 56.

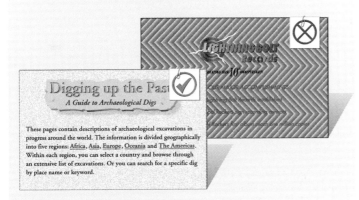

FIND BACKGROUND IMAGES

You can find background images that you can use for free at the following Web sites:

imagine.metanet.com

www.ip.pt/webground/main.htm

www.nepthys.com/textures

You can add a horizontal rule to visually separate sections of your Web page.

ADD A HORIZONTAL RULE

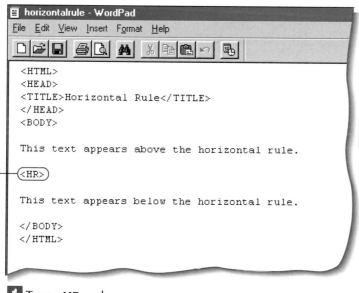

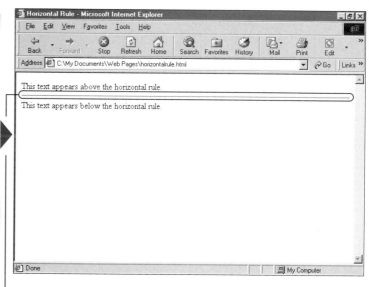

1 Type **<HR>** where you want a horizontal rule to appear on your Web page.

■ The Web browser displays the horizontal rule.

■ To display your Web page in a Web browser, see pages 32 to 35.

How many horizontal rules can I add to my Web page?

You should not overuse horizontal rules on your Web page since this can distract your readers and make your Web page difficult to read. Try not to place more than one horizontal rule on each screen.

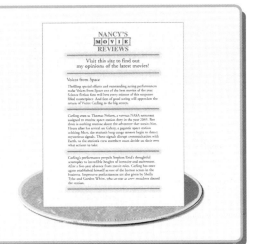

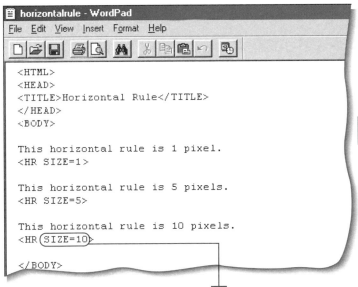

```
📄 horizontalrule - WordPad
File  Edit  View  Insert  Format  Help

<HTML>
<HEAD>
<TITLE>Horizontal Rule</TITLE>
</HEAD>
<BODY>

This horizontal rule is 1 pixel.
<HR SIZE=1>

This horizontal rule is 5 pixels.
<HR SIZE=5>

This horizontal rule is 10 pixels.
<HR SIZE=10>

</BODY>
```

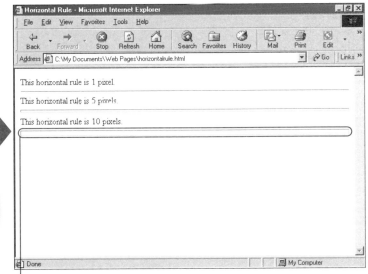

CHANGE THICKNESS

You can change the thickness of a horizontal rule.

■ In the <HR> tag for the horizontal rule you want to change, type **SIZE=?** replacing **?** with the thickness you want to use for the horizontal rule in pixels.

■ The Web browser displays the horizontal rule with the thickness you specified.

■ To display your Web page in a Web browser, see pages 32 to 35.

Note: The SIZE attribute is still supported by Web browsers, but the use of style sheets is now preferred. For information on style sheets, see page 172.

CONTINUED ▶

You can change the width of a horizontal rule if you do not want the rule to extend across the entire Web page.

ADD A HORIZONTAL RULE (CONTINUED)

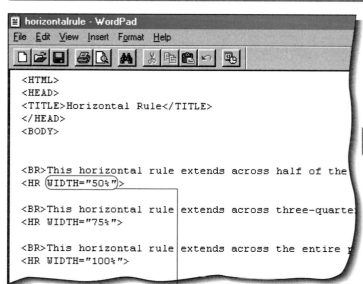

```
<HTML>
<HEAD>
<TITLE>Horizontal Rule</TITLE>
</HEAD>
<BODY>

<BR>This horizontal rule extends across half of the
<HR WIDTH="50%">

<BR>This horizontal rule extends across three-quarte
<HR WIDTH="75%">

<BR>This horizontal rule extends across the entire
<HR WIDTH="100%">
```

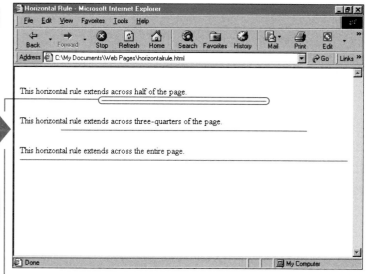

CHANGE WIDTH

You can change the width of a horizontal rule.

1 In the <HR> tag for the horizontal rule you want to change, type **WIDTH="?%"** replacing **?** with the percentage of the Web page you want the horizontal rule to extend across.

*Note: To have the horizontal rule extend halfway across your Web page, type **50**.*

■ The Web browser displays the horizontal rule with the new width. The horizontal rule appears centered on your Web page.

■ To display your Web page in a Web browser, see pages 32 to 35.

Note: The WIDTH attribute is still supported by Web browsers, but the use of style sheets is now preferred. For information on style sheets, see page 172.

How can I add a more elaborate horizontal rule to my Web page?

You can use an image instead of a horizontal rule to visually separate sections of your Web page. You can create your own horizontal rule images in an image editing program or obtain images on the Internet. The following Web sites offer images you can use as horizontal rules:

members.xoom.com/SSWebGraphics/lines/lines.htm

www.coolgraphics.com/gallery.shtml

www.theskull.com/hor_rule.html

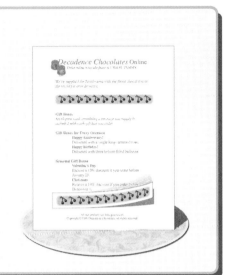

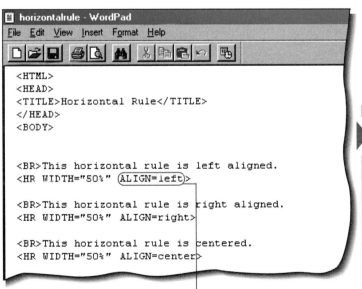

CHANGE ALIGNMENT

After changing the width of a horizontal rule, you can change the alignment of the rule.

■ 1 In the <HR> tag for the horizontal rule you want to change, type **ALIGN=?** replacing **?** with the way you want to align the horizontal rule (**left**, **center** or **right**).

■ The Web browser displays the horizontal rule with the alignment you specified.

■ To display your Web page in a Web browser, see pages 32 to 35.

Note: The ALIGN attribute is still supported by Web browsers, but the use of style sheets is now preferred. For information on style sheets, see page 172.

CHAPTER 6

WORK WITH IMAGES

Are you wondering how to change the appearance of images on your Web pages? This chapter will show you how to change the size of an image, make an image background transparent and much more.

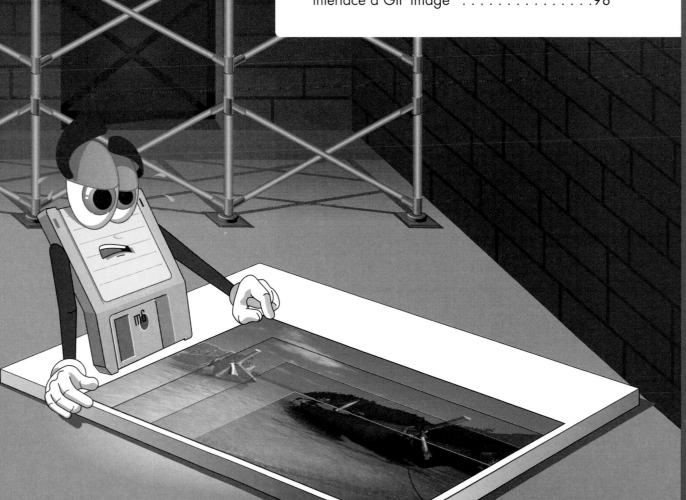

You can convert an image to the GIF or JPEG format. This allows you to display the image on a Web page.

The GIF and JPEG formats are the most popular image formats on the Web.

To convert an image to the GIF or JPEG format, you need an image editing program such as Paint Shop Pro. You can obtain Paint Shop Pro at computer stores or at the www.jasc.com Web site.

CONVERT AN IMAGE TO GIF OR JPEG

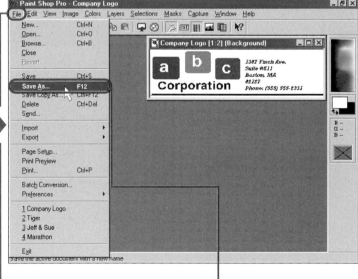

1 Start your image editing program. In this example, we started Paint Shop Pro.

2 Open the image you want to convert to the GIF or JPEG format.

3 Click **File**.

4 Click **Save As**.

TIP

What is the difference between the GIF and JPEG formats?

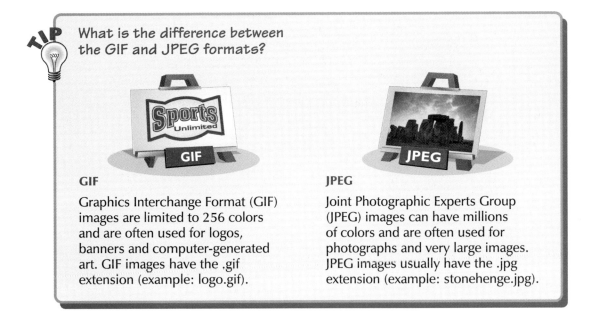

GIF

Graphics Interchange Format (GIF) images are limited to 256 colors and are often used for logos, banners and computer-generated art. GIF images have the .gif extension (example: logo.gif).

JPEG

Joint Photographic Experts Group (JPEG) images can have millions of colors and are often used for photographs and very large images. JPEG images usually have the .jpg extension (example: stonehenge.jpg).

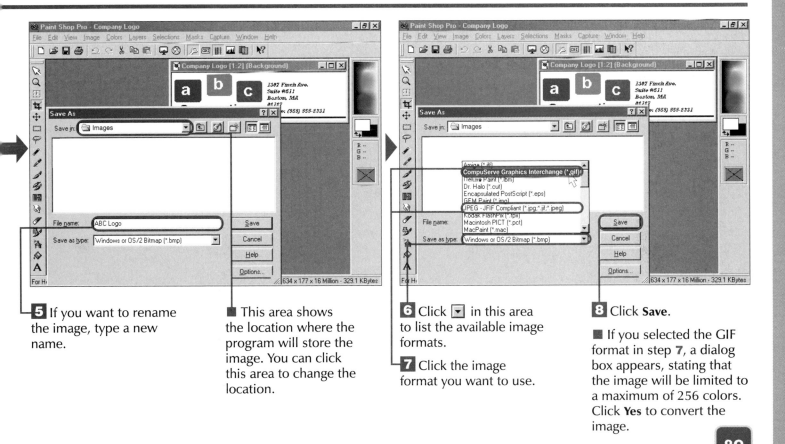

5 If you want to rename the image, type a new name.

■ This area shows the location where the program will store the image. You can click this area to change the location.

6 Click ▼ in this area to list the available image formats.

7 Click the image format you want to use.

8 Click **Save**.

■ If you selected the GIF format in step **7**, a dialog box appears, stating that the image will be limited to a maximum of 256 colors. Click **Yes** to convert the image.

DEFINE IMAGE SIZE

You can define the width and height of an image. Your Web page will appear more quickly since Web browsers do not have to calculate the size of the image.

To determine the size of an image, you need an image editing program such as Paint Shop Pro. You can obtain Paint Shop Pro at computer stores or at the www.jasc.com Web site.

DEFINE IMAGE SIZE

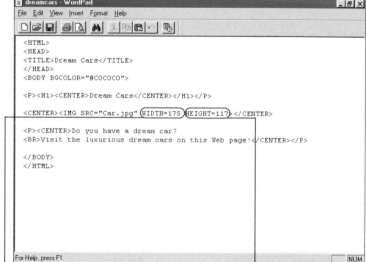

DETERMINE SIZE OF IMAGE

1 Start your image editing program. In this example, we started Paint Shop Pro.

2 Open the image you want to determine the size of.

3 Position the mouse anywhere over the image.

■ This area displays the width and height of the image in pixels.

4 Write down the width and height values on a piece of paper.

DEFINE SIZE OF IMAGE

1 In the <IMG> tag for the image, type **WIDTH=?** replacing **?** with the width of the image in pixels. Then press the **Spacebar**.

2 Type **HEIGHT=?** replacing **?** with the height of the image in pixels.

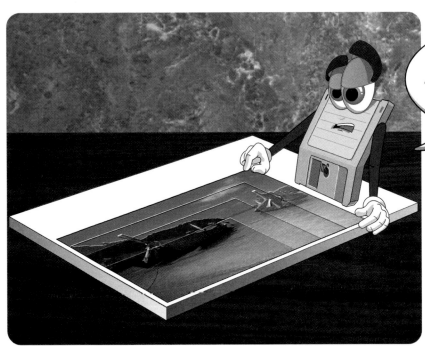

You can increase the size of an image on a Web page by specifying a new width and height for the image.

You should avoid making images too large since the images may appear grainy.

INCREASE IMAGE SIZE

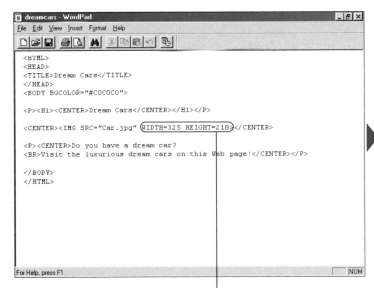

1 Define the size of the image you want to change. To define the size of an image, see page 90.

2 Replace the WIDTH and HEIGHT values with the new width and height you want to use in pixels.

Note: To prevent distorting the image, you should keep the width and height values proportional.

■ The Web browser displays the image with the new size.

■ To display your Web page in a Web browser, see pages 32 to 35.

You can reduce the size of an image so the image will take up less space on your Web page.

To reduce the size of an image, you need an image editing program such as Paint Shop Pro. You can obtain Paint Shop Pro at computer stores or at the www.jasc.com Web site.

REDUCE IMAGE SIZE

1 Start your image editing program. In this example, we started Paint Shop Pro.

2 Open the image you want to resize.

3 Click **Image**.

4 Click **Resize**.

■ The Resize dialog box appears.

5 Click **Pixel Size** (○ changes to ⊙).

6 This area displays the width of the image. Double-click this area and type a new width for the image.

■ The program automatically calculates the height for you to keep the image in proportion.

7 Click **OK** to confirm your changes.

92

TIP

Will reducing the size of an image speed up the display of the image on my Web page?

Yes. Reducing the size of an image decreases the file size of the image. This allows the image to transfer faster and appear on a screen more quickly. Many people link a small version of an image to a larger version of the image. This lets readers quickly view the smaller image and decide if they want to wait to view the larger image. To create a link to a larger image, see page 106.

Barns in the N.W.

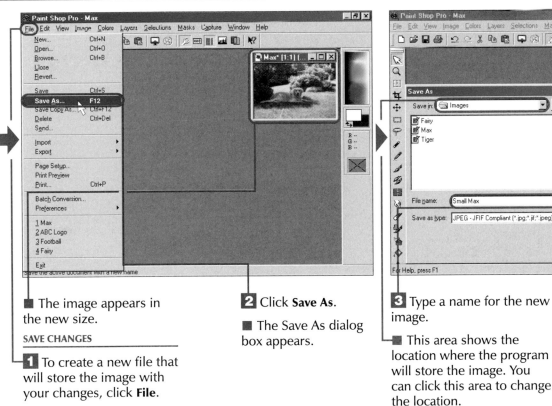

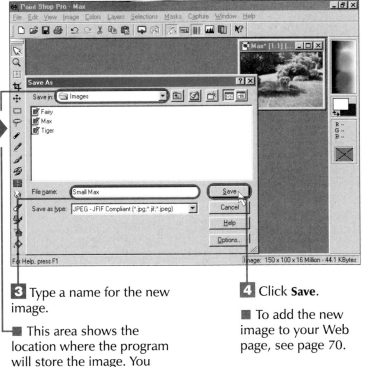

■ The image appears in the new size.

SAVE CHANGES

1 To create a new file that will store the image with your changes, click **File**.

2 Click **Save As**.

■ The Save As dialog box appears.

3 Type a name for the new image.

■ This area shows the location where the program will store the image. You can click this area to change the location.

4 Click **Save**.

■ To add the new image to your Web page, see page 70.

REDUCE COLORS IN AN IMAGE

You can reduce the number of colors in an image. This will decrease the file size of the image so the image can transfer more quickly over the Internet.

To reduce the number of colors in an image, you need an image editing program such as Paint Shop Pro. You can obtain Paint Shop Pro at computer stores or at the www.jasc.com Web site.

REDUCE COLORS IN AN IMAGE

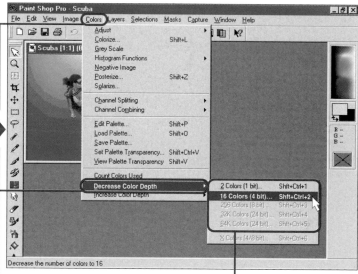

1 Start your image editing program. In this example, we started Paint Shop Pro.

2 Open the image you want to change.

Note: You should not reduce the number of colors in a JPEG image. For more information, see the top of page 95.

3 Click **Colors**.

4 Click **Decrease Color Depth**.

5 Click the number of colors you want the image to contain.

Can I reduce the number of colors in a JPEG image?

You should not reduce the number of colors in a JPEG image. The JPEG format was specifically designed to store images containing millions of colors using small file sizes. In many cases, reducing the number of colors in a JPEG image will increase the file size of the image.

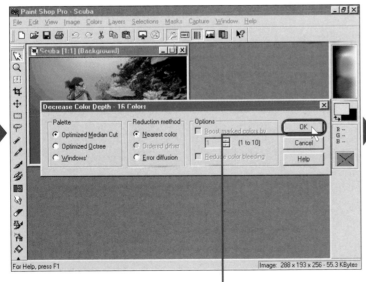

■ The Decrease Color Depth dialog box appears.

Note: The dialog box that appears on your screen may offer different options.

6 Click **OK** to confirm your change.

■ The image displays the new number of colors.

7 To create a new file that will store the image with the new number of colors, perform steps **1** to **4** on page 93.

■ To add the new image to your Web page, see page 70.

You can make the background of a GIF image transparent so the background will blend into a Web page.

To make the background of a GIF image transparent, you need an image editing program such as Paint Shop Pro. You can obtain Paint Shop Pro at computer stores or at the www.jasc.com Web site.

MAKE IMAGE BACKGROUND TRANSPARENT

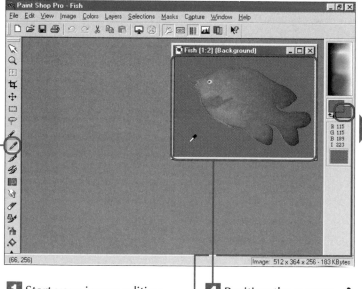

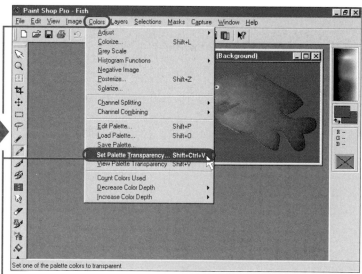

1 Start your image editing program. In this example, we started Paint Shop Pro.

2 Open the GIF image you want to change.

3 Click ✎.

4 Position the mouse ✐ over the background area of the image. Then click the **right** mouse button.

■ This area displays the color you selected.

5 Click **Colors**.

6 Click **Set Palette Transparency**.

■ The Set Palette Transparency dialog box appears.

What should I consider when making the background of an image transparent?

Single Background Color

Choose images with a single background color. If an image has a multicolored background, only one of the colors in the background will become transparent.

Different Background Color

Make sure the background color does not appear in the image itself. When you make the background of an image transparent, every part of the image that displays the same color as the background will also become transparent.

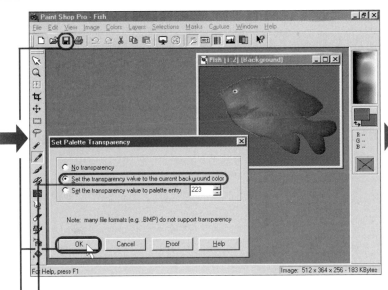

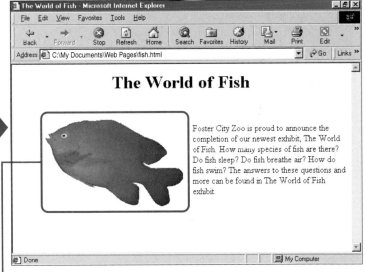

7 Click this option (○ changes to ⊙).

8 Click **OK** to confirm your selection.

9 Click 🖫 to save your change.

■ The background of the image does not appear transparent in the image editing program, but will appear transparent on a Web page.

■ To add the image to a Web page, see page 70.

■ The Web browser displays the image with a transparent background.

■ To display your Web page in a Web browser, see pages 32 to 35.

■ If you no longer want to display the image with a transparent background, repeat steps **1** to **9**, selecting **No transparency** in step **7**.

You can interlace a GIF image. An interlaced GIF image first appears blurry and then gradually sharpens as it transfers to a computer.

To interlace a GIF image, you need an image editing program such as Paint Shop Pro. You can obtain Paint Shop Pro at computer stores or at the www.jasc.com Web site.

INTERLACE A GIF IMAGE

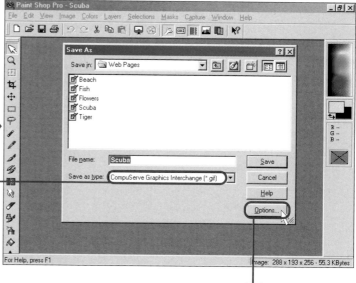

1 Start your image editing program. In this example, we started Paint Shop Pro.

2 Open the GIF image you want to interlace.

3 Click **File**.

4 Click **Save As**.

■ The Save As dialog box appears.

■ This area displays the image type. Make sure the image is a GIF image.

5 Click **Options**.

Why should I interlace a GIF image?

An interlaced GIF image will appear on the screen as it transfers to a computer. This gives your readers some idea of what the final Web page will look like. Noninterlaced images must fully transfer to a computer before appearing on the screen. This leaves readers unsure of what the final Web page will look like.

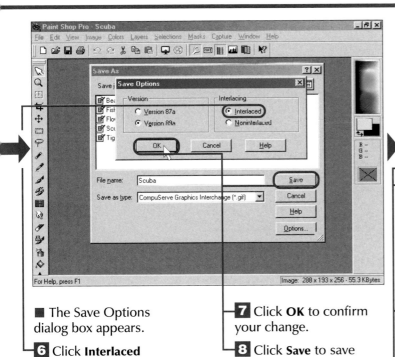

■ The Save Options dialog box appears.

6 Click **Interlaced** (○ changes to ⊙).

7 Click **OK** to confirm your change.

8 Click **Save** to save your change.

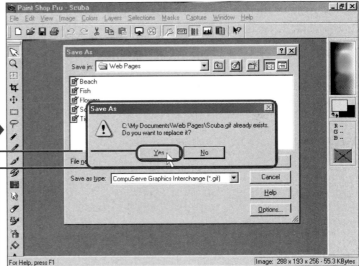

■ A dialog box appears, stating that you will replace the original image.

9 Click **Yes** to replace the original image.

■ The image is now interlaced. To add the image to your Web page, see page 70.

*Note: To remove interlacing from an image, repeat steps 1 to 9, selecting **Noninterlaced** in step 6.*

Science Today

CHAPTER 7

CREATE LINKS

Are you wondering how to create links that will connect your Web pages to other information on the Internet? This chapter shows you how.

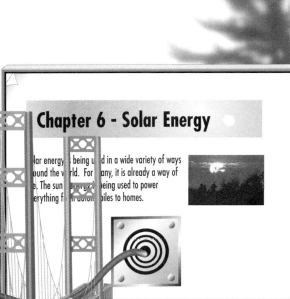

Chapter 6 - Solar Energy

Solar energy is being used in a wide variety of ways around the world. For many, it is already a way of life. The sun energy is being used to power everything from automobiles to homes.

(125K)

(130K)

(116K)

(105K)

(115K)

(120K)

CREATE A LINK TO ANOTHER WEB PAGE

You can link a word, phrase or image on your Web page to another page on the Web.

You can create a link to a Web page in your own Web site or to any page on the Web.

CREATE A TEXT LINK

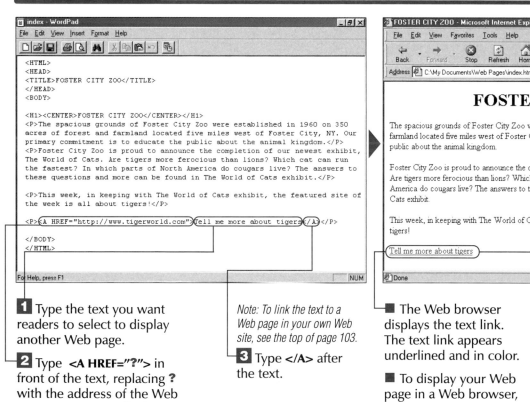

1 Type the text you want readers to select to display another Web page.

2 Type **<A HREF="?">** in front of the text, replacing **?** with the address of the Web page you want to display.

Note: To link the text to a Web page in your own Web site, see the top of page 103.

3 Type **</A>** after the text.

■ The Web browser displays the text link. The text link appears underlined and in color.

■ To display your Web page in a Web browser, see pages 32 to 35.

■ A reader can click the text link to display the Web page you specified.

How do I create a link to a Web page in my own Web site?

The Web pages in your Web site should be stored in one folder on your computer. If the folder contains many Web pages, you can store some pages in a subfolder.

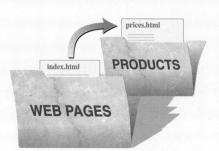

To create a link to a Web page that is stored in the same folder, you can specify just the name of the Web page (example: prices.html).

To create a link to a Web page that is stored in a subfolder, you must specify the name of the subfolder and the name of the Web page (example: products/prices.html).

CREATE AN IMAGE LINK

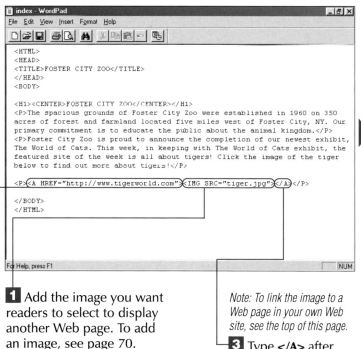
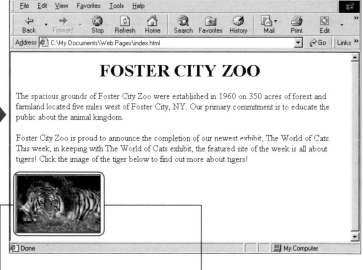

1 Add the image you want readers to select to display another Web page. To add an image, see page 70.

2 Type **<A HREF="?">** in front of the image, replacing **?** with the address of the Web page you want to display.

Note: To link the image to a Web page in your own Web site, see the top of this page.

3 Type **</A>** after the image.

■ The Web browser displays the image link. A border appears around the image link.

Note: To remove a border from an image, see page 73.

■ To display your Web page in a Web browser, see pages 32 to 35.

■ A reader can click the image link to display the Web page you specified.

103

CREATE A LINK WITHIN A WEB PAGE

You can create a link that will take readers to another area of a long Web page. This lets readers quickly display information of interest.

For example, you can create a table of contents that contains links to different sections of a long Web page.

CREATE A LINK WITHIN A WEB PAGE

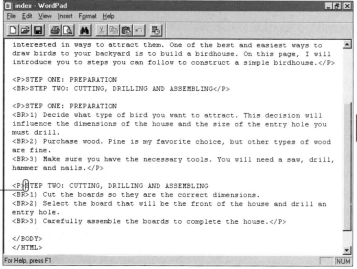

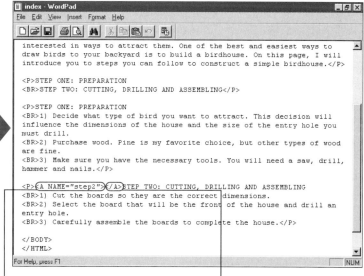

NAME WEB PAGE AREA

1 Position the cursor in front of the Web page area you want readers to be able to quickly display.

2 Type **<A NAME="?">** replacing **?** with a name that describes the Web page area. The name you use should contain only letters and numbers (A to Z and 0 to 9).

3 Type **</A>** to complete the naming of the Web page area.

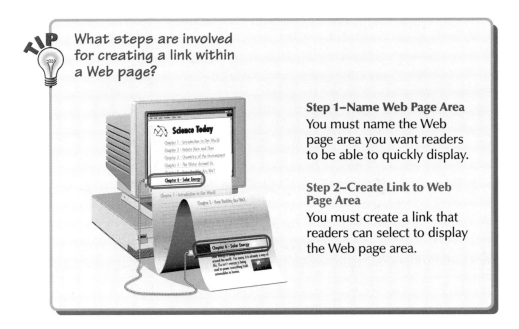

TIP

What steps are involved for creating a link within a Web page?

Step 1–Name Web Page Area
You must name the Web page area you want readers to be able to quickly display.

Step 2–Create Link to Web Page Area
You must create a link that readers can select to display the Web page area.

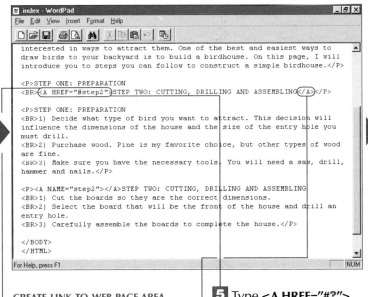

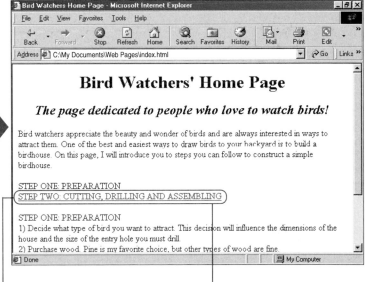

CREATE LINK TO WEB PAGE AREA

4 Position the cursor in front of the text or image you want readers to select to display the Web page area you named on page 104.

5 Type **<A HREF="#?">** replacing **?** with the name you specified for the Web page area in step **2**.

6 Type **</A>** after the text or image.

■ The Web browser displays the link.

■ To display your Web page in a Web browser, see pages 32 to 35.

■ A reader can click the link to display the Web page area you specified.

You can create a link on your Web page that will take readers to an image.

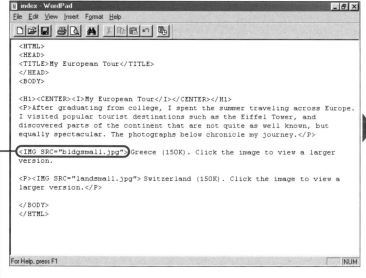

For example, you can link a small version of an image to a larger version of the image. This lets readers decide if they want to wait to view the larger image. To create a smaller version of an image, see page 92.

CREATE A LINK TO AN IMAGE

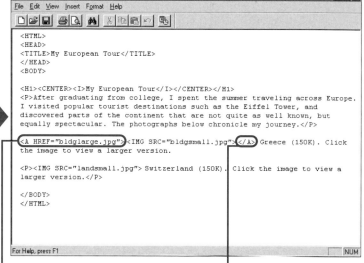

```
index - WordPad                                    _ 8 X
File  Edit  View  Insert  Format  Help

<HTML>
<HEAD>
<TITLE>My European Tour</TITLE>
</HEAD>
<BODY>

<H1><CENTER><I>My European Tour</I></CENTER></H1>
<P>After graduating from college, I spent the summer traveling across Europe.
I visited popular tourist destinations such as the Eiffel Tower, and
discovered parts of the continent that are not quite as well known, but
equally spectacular. The photographs below chronicle my journey.</P>

<IMG SRC="bldgsmall.jpg">Greece (150K). Click the image to view a larger
version.

<P><IMG SRC="landsmall.jpg"> Switzerland (150K). Click the image to view a
larger version.</P>

</BODY>
</HTML>

For Help, press F1                                      NUM
```

```
index - WordPad                                    _ 8 X
File  Edit  View  Insert  Format  Help

<HTML>
<HEAD>
<TITLE>My European Tour</TITLE>
</HEAD>
<BODY>

<H1><CENTER><I>My European Tour</I></CENTER></H1>
<P>After graduating from college, I spent the summer traveling across Europe.
I visited popular tourist destinations such as the Eiffel Tower, and
discovered parts of the continent that are not quite as well known, but
equally spectacular. The photographs below chronicle my journey.</P>

<A HREF="bldglarge.jpg"><IMG SRC="bldgsmall.jpg"></A> Greece (150K). Click
the image to view a larger version.

<P><IMG SRC="landsmall.jpg"> Switzerland (150K). Click the image to view a
larger version.</P>

</BODY>
</HTML>

For Help, press F1                                      NUM
```

1 Type the text or add the image you want readers to select to display the linked image. To add an image, see page 70.

2 Type **<A HREF="?">** in front of the text or image, replacing **?** with the location of the linked image on your computer.

Note: For information on specifying the location of an image, see page 71.

3 Type **</A>** after the text or image.

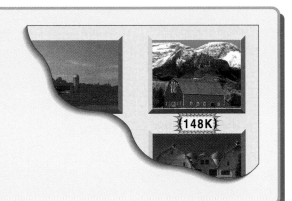

What should I consider when creating a link to an image?

You should consider including the size of the linked image in kilobytes (K) beside the link. This can help readers determine how long the linked image will take to transfer to their computer.

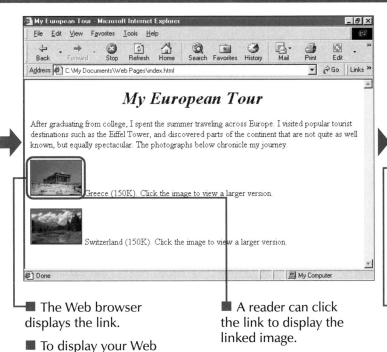

■ The Web browser displays the link.

■ To display your Web page in a Web browser, see pages 32 to 35.

■ A reader can click the link to display the linked image.

■ When a reader selects the link, the image you specified appears.

You can create a link that allows readers to quickly send you an e-mail message.

CREATE AN E-MAIL LINK

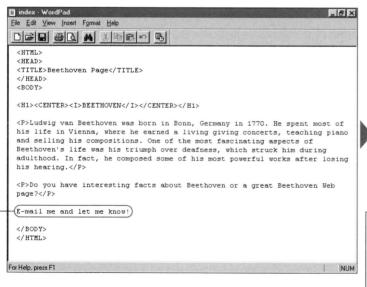

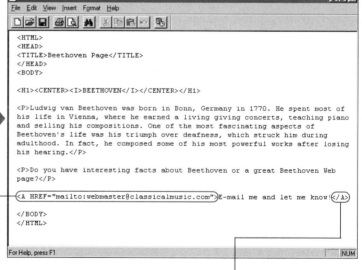

1 Type the text or add the image you want readers to select to send you an e-mail message. To add an image, see page 70.

2 Type **<A HREF="mailto:?">** in front of the text or image, replacing **?** with the e-mail address of the person you want to receive the messages.

3 Type **</A>** after the text or image.

Why should I include an e-mail link on my Web page?

An e-mail link allows readers to send you questions and provide feedback that can help improve your Web pages. Many companies include a list of e-mail links that allow you to contact employees in different departments. This helps readers determine which person they should send an e-mail message to.

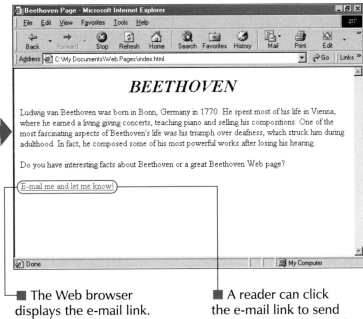

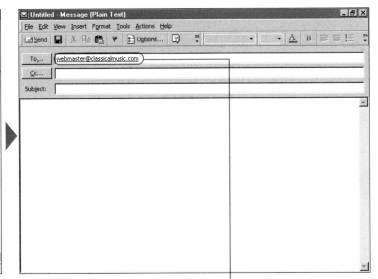

■ The Web browser displays the e-mail link.

■ To display your Web page in a Web browser, see pages 32 to 35.

■ A reader can click the e-mail link to send a message to the e-mail address you specified.

■ When a reader selects an e-mail link, the reader's e-mail program will start.

■ The e-mail program will automatically display the e-mail address you specified to ensure the message will reach the correct person.

An unvisited link is a link a reader has not previously selected. A visited link is a link a reader has previously selected.

CHANGE UNVISITED LINKS

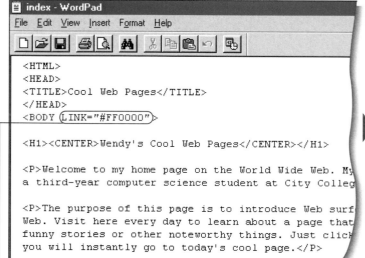

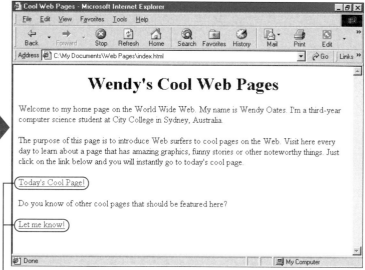

1 In the <BODY> tag, type **LINK="?"** replacing **?** with the name or code for the color you want to use (example: red or #FF0000).

Note: For a list of colors, see the top of page 57.

■ The Web browser displays the unvisited links in the color you selected.

■ To display your Web page in a Web browser, see pages 32 to 35.

Note: The LINK attribute is still supported by Web browsers, but the use of style sheets is now preferred. For information on style sheets, see page 172.

What should I consider when changing the color of links?

Make sure you choose different colors for unvisited and visited links. The colors should work well with the background color of your Web page.

Unvisited
Visited

The colors you choose for links may not appear the way you expect on some computers. Readers can set their Web browsers to override the colors you choose.

CHANGE VISITED LINKS

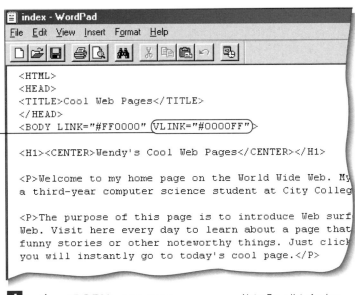

```
<HTML>
<HEAD>
<TITLE>Cool Web Pages</TITLE>
</HEAD>
<BODY LINK="#FF0000" VLINK="#0000FF">

<H1><CENTER>Wendy's Cool Web Pages</CENTER></H1>

<P>Welcome to my home page on the World Wide Web. My
a third-year computer science student at City Colleg

<P>The purpose of this page is to introduce Web surf
Web. Visit here every day to learn about a page that
funny stories or other noteworthy things. Just click
you will instantly go to today's cool page.</P>
```

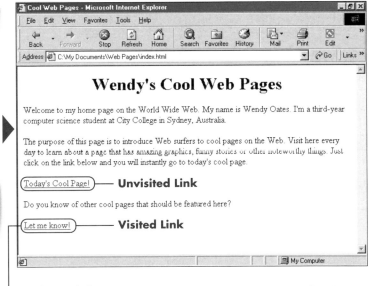

1 In the <BODY> tag, type **VLINK="?"** replacing **?** with the name or code for the color you want to use (example: blue or #0000FF).

Note: For a list of colors, see the top of page 57.

■ The Web browser displays the visited link in the color you selected.

■ To display your Web page in a Web browser, see pages 32 to 35.

Note: The VLINK attribute is still supported by Web browsers, but the use of style sheets is now preferred. For information on style sheets, see page 172.

BE DESCRIPTIVE

Make sure the text or image you use for a link clearly indicates where the link will take your readers. Do not use the phrase "Click Here" for a link, since this phrase is not very informative.

INCLUDE TEXT LINKS

If your Web page contains image links, you should provide corresponding text links for your readers. Some readers turn off the display of images to browse the Web more quickly, while others use Web browsers that cannot display images. You can include text links beside image links or in a list at the bottom of your Web page.

SEPARATE LINKS

Do not place two text links beside each other on your Web page. When two text links appear side by side, readers may find it difficult to see there are two separate links, as opposed to one long link.

USE LINK MENUS

If you plan to include many links on your Web page, you should consider displaying the links in a menu format, like a table of contents in a book.

CHECK YOUR LINKS

If your Web page contains links to Web pages you did not create, you should verify the links on a regular basis. You will frustrate readers who select a link that no longer contains relevant information or displays an error message.

USE DEFINITION LINKS

If your Web page contains technical terms that readers may not understand, you should consider including definition links that will take readers to brief explanations of the terms.

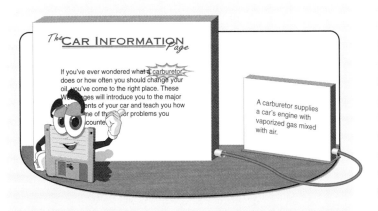

NOTIFY READERS OF TRANSFER TIME

Let readers know about any links that will take them to Web pages or images that will take a long time to transfer. This allows readers to decide if they want to select the link.

USE NAVIGATIONAL LINKS

You should include navigational links on your Web pages to help readers move through your pages. Each Web page should include a link to your home page. You can find images for navigational links at the following Web sites:

www.freeimages.com

www.classic-themes.freeserve.co.uk

www.iconbazaar.com

Team	Games	Wins	Losses	Ties	Points
The Chargers	10	9	1	0	18
Sluggers	10	8	1	1	17
The Champs	10	7	2	1	15
The Eagles	10	5	5	0	10
Barry's Battalion	10	3	7	0	6
The Professionals	10	2	8	0	4
Baseball Bombers	10	1	9	0	2

CHAPTER 8

CREATE TABLES

Are you interested in using tables to organize information on your Web pages? Read this chapter to learn how.

Softball Standings

Team	Games	Wins	Losses	Ties	Points
The Chargers	10	9	1	0	18
Sluggers	10	8	1	1	17
The Champs	10	7	2	1	15
The Eagles	10	5	5	0	10
Barry's Battalion	10	3	7	0	6
The Professionals	10	2	8	0	4
Baseball Bombers	10	1	9	0	2

Pool A

Team	Games	Wins	Loss	Ti
The Chargers	10	9	1	0
Sluggers	10	8	1	1
The Champs	10	7	2	
The Eagles	10	5	5	

You can create a table to neatly display information on a Web page.

Softball Standings

Team	Games	Wins	Losses	Ties	Points
The Chargers	10	9	1	0	18
Sluggers	10	8	1	1	17
The Champs	10	7	2	1	15
The Eagles	10	5	5	0	10
Barry's Battalion	10	3	7	0	6
The Professionals	10	2	8	0	4
Baseball Bombers	10	1	9	0	2

You can use the PREFORMAT tag to quickly create a simple table. For more information on the PREFORMAT tag, see page 42.

CREATE A TABLE

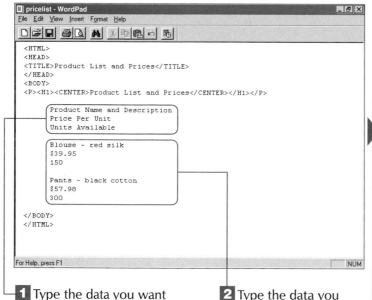

```
pricelist - WordPad
File  Edit  View  Insert  Format  Help

<HTML>
<HEAD>
<TITLE>Product List and Prices</TITLE>
</HEAD>
<BODY>
<P><H1><CENTER>Product List and Prices</CENTER></H1></P>

        Product Name and Description
        Price Per Unit
        Units Available

        Blouse - red silk
        $39.95
        150

        Pants - black cotton
        $57.98
        300

</BODY>
</HTML>

For Help, press F1                                    NUM
```

```
pricelist - WordPad
File  Edit  View  Insert  Format  Help

<HTML>
<HEAD>
<TITLE>Product List and Prices</TITLE>
</HEAD>
<BODY>
<P><H1><CENTER>Product List and Prices</CENTER></H1></P>
<TABLE>
<TR>
        Product Name and Description
        Price Per Unit
        Units Available
</TR>
<TR>
        Blouse - red silk
        $39.95
        150
</TR>
<TR>
        Pants - black cotton
        $57.98
        300
</TR>
</TABLE>
</BODY>

For Help, press F1                                    NUM
```

1 Type the data you want to appear in the first row of the table.

■ You can use the `Enter` and `Tab` keys to visually separate the data for each cell. The Web browser will ignore the spacing you add.

2 Type the data you want to appear in the next row of the table. Repeat this step until you finish entering all the data for the table.

3 Type **<TABLE>** before the text you entered for the table.

4 Type **</TABLE>** after the text you entered for the table.

5 Type **<TR>** before the text for each row in the table.

6 Type **</TR>** after the text for each row in the table.

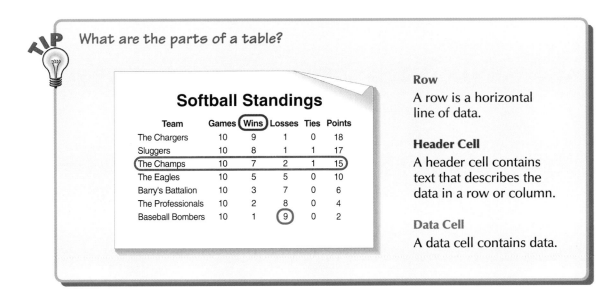

What are the parts of a table?

Softball Standings

Team	Games	Wins	Losses	Ties	Points
The Chargers	10	9	1	0	18
Sluggers	10	8	1	1	17
The Champs	10	7	2	1	15
The Eagles	10	5	5	0	10
Barry's Battalion	10	3	7	0	6
The Professionals	10	2	8	0	4
Baseball Bombers	10	1	9	0	2

Row

A row is a horizontal line of data.

Header Cell

A header cell contains text that describes the data in a row or column.

Data Cell

A data cell contains data.

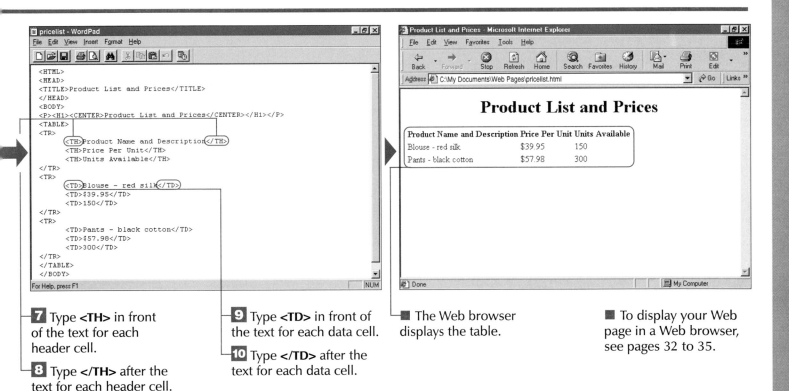

7 Type **<TH>** in front of the text for each header cell.

8 Type **</TH>** after the text for each header cell.

9 Type **<TD>** in front of the text for each data cell.

10 Type **</TD>** after the text for each data cell.

■ The Web browser displays the table.

■ To display your Web page in a Web browser, see pages 32 to 35.

REASONS FOR USING TABLES

DISPLAY LISTS OF INFORMATION

Tables provide a great way to neatly display lists of information on your Web pages. For example, you can use tables to display financial data and price lists.

CREATE NEWSPAPER COLUMNS

You can use tables to present information in columns like those found in a newspaper. To display information in three newspaper columns, you can create a table with one row that contains three cells.

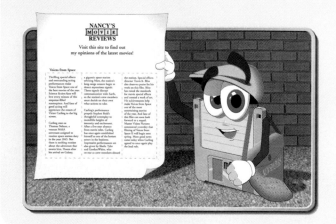

CONTROL WEB PAGE LAYOUT

Tables are useful for controlling the placement of text and images on your Web pages. To neatly position two paragraphs and two images, you can create a table with two rows that contain two cells each.

CREATE BORDERS

You can use a table to place a three-dimensional border around text or an image on your Web page. To place a 3-D border around text or an image, place the text or image in a table with one row that contains one cell.

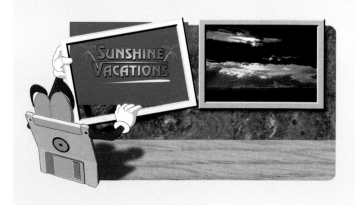

You can center a table to improve the overall appearance of your Web page.

CENTER A TABLE

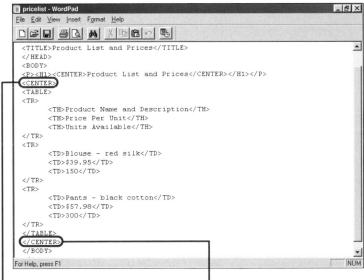

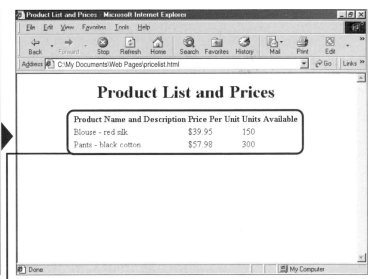

1 Type **<CENTER>** directly above the <TABLE> tag.

2 Type **</CENTER>** directly below the </TABLE> tag.

■ The Web browser centers the table on your Web page.

■ To display your Web page in a Web browser, see pages 32 to 35.

Note: The CENTER tag is still supported by Web browsers, but the use of style sheets is now preferred. For information on style sheets, see page 172.

> You can add a border to a table to separate each cell in the table. This will make the data in the table easier to read.

Team	Games	Wins	Losses	Ties	Points
The Chargers	10	9	1	0	18
Sluggers	10	8	1	1	17
The Champs	10	7	2	1	15
The Eagles	10	5	5	0	10
Barry's Battalion	10	3	7	0	6
The Professionals	10	2	8	0	4
Baseball Bombers	10	1	9	0	2

ADD A BORDER

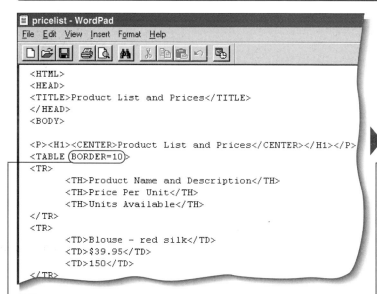

```
<HTML>
<HEAD>
<TITLE>Product List and Prices</TITLE>
</HEAD>
<BODY>

<P><H1><CENTER>Product List and Prices</CENTER></H1></P>
<TABLE BORDER=10>
<TR>
        <TH>Product Name and Description</TH>
        <TH>Price Per Unit</TH>
        <TH>Units Available</TH>
</TR>
<TR>
        <TD>Blouse - red silk</TD>
        <TD>$39.95</TD>
        <TD>150</TD>
</TR>
```

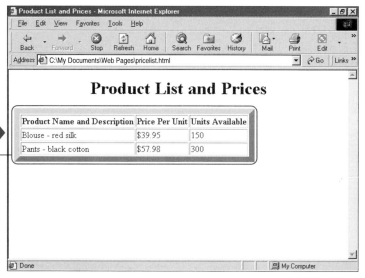

1 In the <TABLE> tag for the table you want to display a border, type **BORDER=?** replacing **?** with the thickness you want to use for the border in pixels.

■ The Web browser displays the table with a border.

■ To display your Web page in a Web browser, see pages 32 to 35.

You can add a caption to summarize the information in a table.

ADD A CAPTION

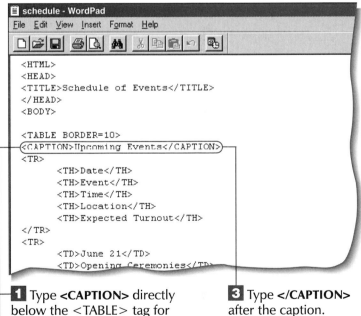

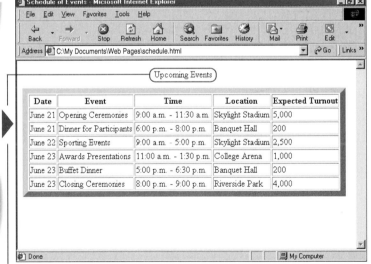

1 Type **<CAPTION>** directly below the <TABLE> tag for the table you want to display a caption.

2 Type the caption you want the table to display.

3 Type **</CAPTION>** after the caption.

■ The Web browser displays the caption above the table.

■ To display your Web page in a Web browser, see pages 32 to 35.

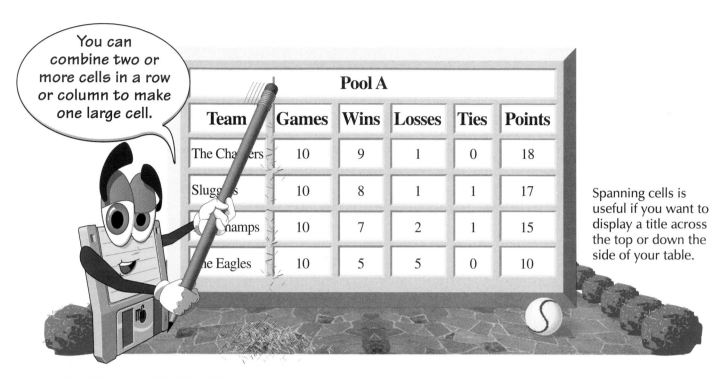

You can combine two or more cells in a row or column to make one large cell.

Spanning cells is useful if you want to display a title across the top or down the side of your table.

SPAN CELLS ACROSS COLUMNS

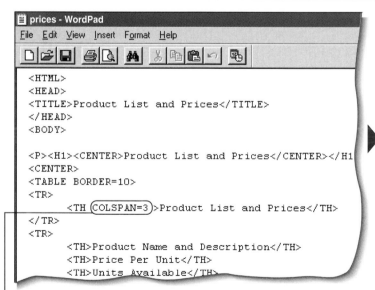

```
<HTML>
<HEAD>
<TITLE>Product List and Prices</TITLE>
</HEAD>
<BODY>

<P><H1><CENTER>Product List and Prices</CENTER></H1
<CENTER>
<TABLE BORDER=10>
<TR>
        <TH COLSPAN=3>Product List and Prices</TH>
</TR>
<TR>
        <TH>Product Name and Description</TH>
        <TH>Price Per Unit</TH>
        <TH>Units Available</TH>
```

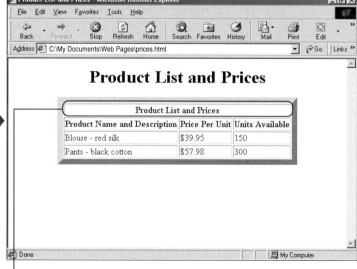

1 In the <TH> or <TD> tag for the cell you want to span across columns, type **COLSPAN=?** replacing **?** with the number of columns you want the cell to span across.

■ The Web browser spans the cell across the number of columns you specified.

■ To display your Web page in a Web browser, see pages 32 to 35.

TIP

How can I prevent problems when spanning cells in a table?

You can prevent problems by sketching your table on a piece of paper before you begin. This allows you to clearly see the layout of your table and can help you avoid errors when spanning cells.

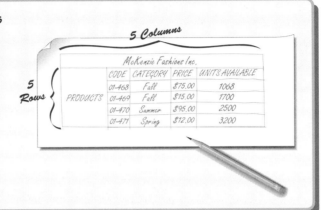

SPAN CELLS DOWN ROWS

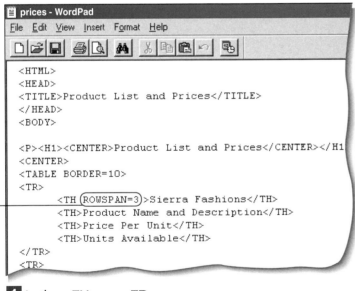

```
<HTML>
<HEAD>
<TITLE>Product List and Prices</TITLE>
</HEAD>
<BODY>

<P><H1><CENTER>Product List and Prices</CENTER></H1
<CENTER>
<TABLE BORDER=10>
<TR>
        <TH ROWSPAN=3>Sierra Fashions</TH>
        <TH>Product Name and Description</TH>
        <TH>Price Per Unit</TH>
        <TH>Units Available</TH>
</TR>
<TR>
```

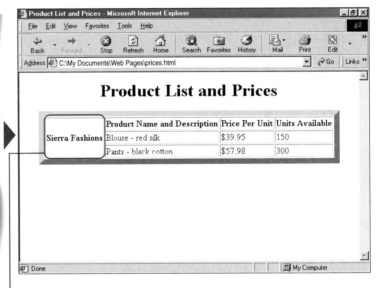

1 In the <TH> or <TD> tag for the cell you want to span down rows, type **ROWSPAN=?** replacing **?** with the number of rows you want the cell to span down.

■ The Web browser spans the cell down the number of rows you specified.

■ To display your Web page in a Web browser, see pages 32 to 35.

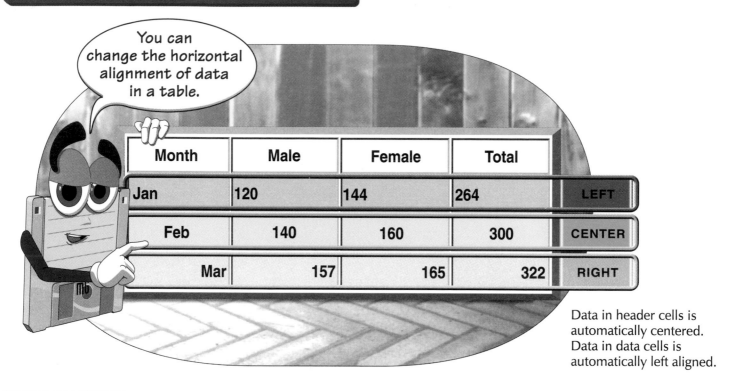

You can change the horizontal alignment of data in a table.

Month	Male	Female	Total	
Jan	120	144	264	LEFT
Feb	140	160	300	CENTER
Mar	157	165	322	RIGHT

Data in header cells is automatically centered. Data in data cells is automatically left aligned.

ALIGN DATA HORIZONTALLY

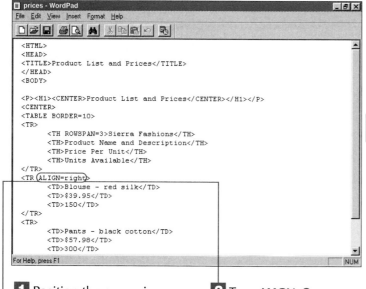

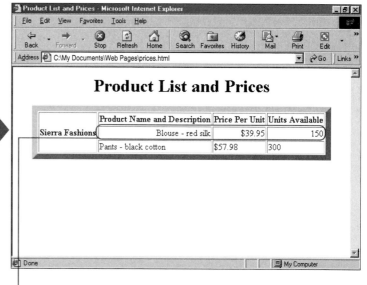

■ **1** Position the cursor in the <TR> tag for the row containing the data you want to align horizontally.

■ **2** Type **ALIGN=?** replacing **?** with the way you want to align the data (**left**, **center** or **right**).

■ The Web browser displays all the data in the row with the alignment you specified.

■ To display your Web page in a Web browser, see pages 32 to 35.

■ To align data horizontally in a single cell, perform step **2** in the <TH> or <TD> tag for the cell.

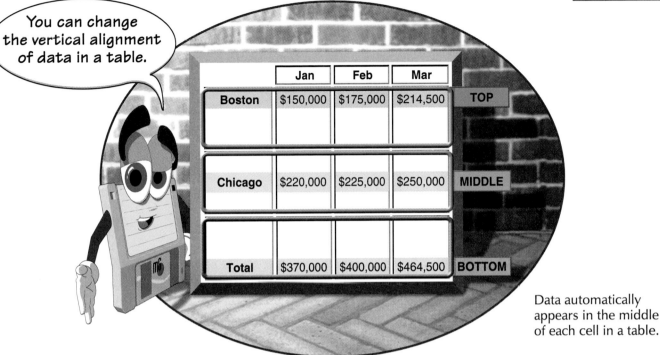

You can change the vertical alignment of data in a table.

	Jan	Feb	Mar	
Boston	$150,000	$175,000	$214,500	TOP
Chicago	$220,000	$225,000	$250,000	MIDDLE
Total	$370,000	$400,000	$464,500	BOTTOM

Data automatically appears in the middle of each cell in a table.

ALIGN DATA VERTICALLY

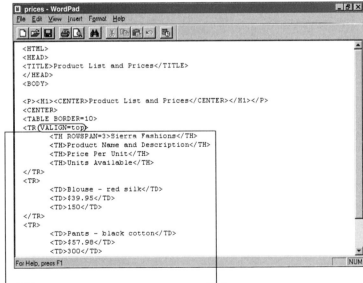

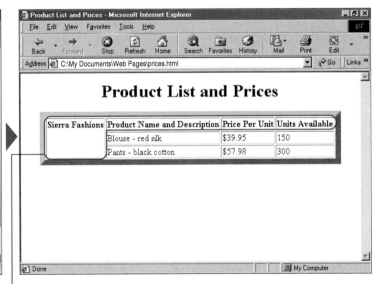

1 Position the cursor in the <TR> tag for the row containing the data you want to align vertically.

2 Type **VALIGN=?** replacing **?** with the way you want to align the data (**top**, **middle** or **bottom**).

■ The Web browser displays all the data in the row with the alignment you specified.

■ To display your Web page in a Web browser, see pages 32 to 35.

■ To align data vertically in a single cell, perform step **2** in the <TH> or <TD> tag for the cell.

Form

What is your age?

○ Under 21   ○ 21-30   ○ 31- 40   ○ Over 40

What state do you live in?

○ Florida   ○ California   ○ New York

Comments

CHAPTER 9

CREATE FORMS

Would you like to create forms that your readers can use to send you information? Find out how in this chapter.

Forms allow you to gather information from readers who visit your Web pages.

QUESTIONS/COMMENTS ABOUT OUR WEB SITE

How did you find out about our Web site?
TV   Newspaper   Friend   Other

Overall, how would you rate our Web site?
Excellent   Very Good   Good   Needs Work

What section in our Web site did you like the most?

What section in our Web site did you like the least?

Comments/Questions:

You can create a form that lets readers send you questions or comments about your Web pages. You can also create a form that allows readers to purchase your products and services on the Web.

HOW FORMS WORK

GATHER INFORMATION

A reader can enter information and select options on a form. When a reader clicks the Submit button, the information transfers to a Web server.

PROCESS INFORMATION

When a Web server receives information from a form, the server runs a program called a Common Gateway Interface (CGI) script that processes the information. The CGI script you use determines how the information is processed. For example, a CGI script can send you the results of a form in an e-mail message, save the results in a document or add the results to a database stored on the Web server.

Before including forms on your Web pages, make sure you can run CGI scripts on your Web server.

You must set up a form before you can add information to the form.

SET UP A FORM

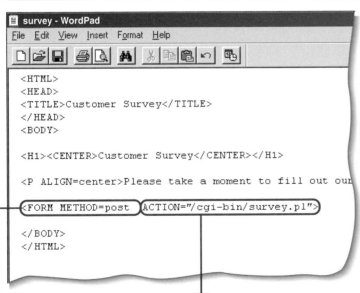

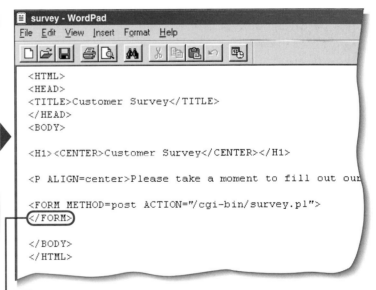

1 Type **<FORM METHOD=post** where you want the form to appear on your Web page. Then press the **Spacebar**.

2 Type **ACTION="?">** replacing **?** with the location of the CGI script on your Web server that will process the information submitted by the form.

Note: To determine the location of the CGI script on your Web server, contact your Web server administrator.

3 Type **</FORM>** to complete the form.

■ You have now set up a form on your Web page. To add information to the form, see pages 130 to 139.

CREATE A TEXT BOX

You can create a text box that allows readers to enter a line of text. Text boxes are commonly used for names and addresses.

CREATE A TEXT BOX

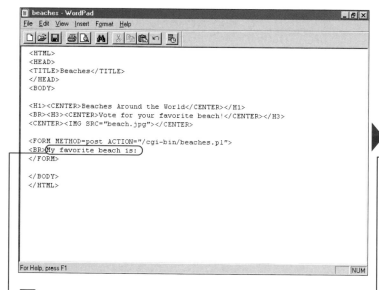

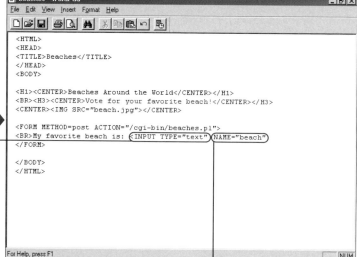

1 Between the <FORM> and </FORM> tags, type the text you want to appear beside the text box. Then press the **Spacebar**.

Note: If you want the text box to appear on its own line, use the P or BR tag. For more information, see pages 36 and 38.

2 Type **<INPUT TYPE="text"** and then press the **Spacebar**.

3 Type **NAME="?"** replacing **?** with a word that describes the text box. Then press the **Spacebar**.

*Note: The text you enter in step **3** identifies the text box to the Web server and will not appear on your Web page.*

130

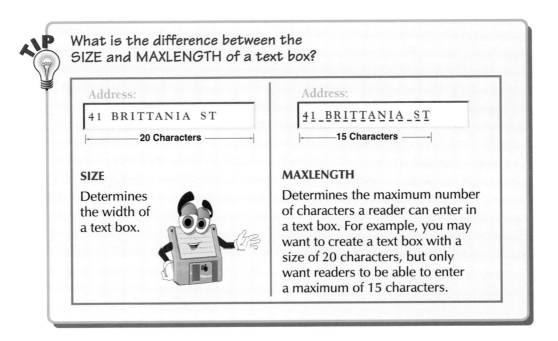

TIP

What is the difference between the SIZE and MAXLENGTH of a text box?

Address:

41 BRITTANIA ST

|— 20 Characters —|

Address:

41 BRITTANIA ST

|— 15 Characters —|

SIZE

Determines the width of a text box.

MAXLENGTH

Determines the maximum number of characters a reader can enter in a text box. For example, you may want to create a text box with a size of 20 characters, but only want readers to be able to enter a maximum of 15 characters.

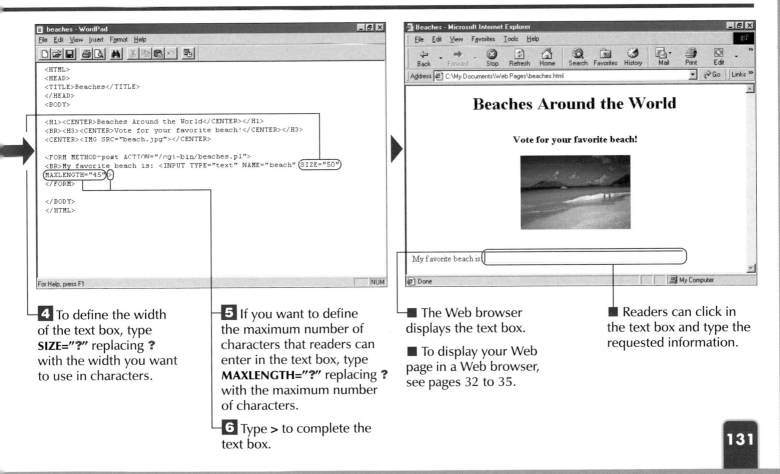

4 To define the width of the text box, type **SIZE="?"** replacing **?** with the width you want to use in characters.

5 If you want to define the maximum number of characters that readers can enter in the text box, type **MAXLENGTH="?"** replacing **?** with the maximum number of characters.

6 Type **>** to complete the text box.

■ The Web browser displays the text box.

■ To display your Web page in a Web browser, see pages 32 to 35.

■ Readers can click in the text box and type the requested information.

CREATE A LARGE TEXT AREA

You can create a large text area that allows readers to enter several lines or paragraphs of text.

A large text area is ideal for gathering comments or questions from your readers.

CREATE A LARGE TEXT AREA

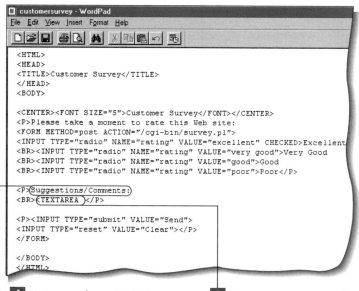

```
customersurvey - WordPad
File  Edit  View  Insert  Format  Help

<HTML>
<HEAD>
<TITLE>Customer Survey</TITLE>
</HEAD>
<BODY>

<CENTER><FONT SIZE="5">Customer Survey</FONT></CENTER>
<P>Please take a moment to rate this Web site:
<FORM METHOD=post ACTION="/cgi-bin/survey.pl">
<INPUT TYPE="radio" NAME="rating" VALUE="excellent" CHECKED>Excellent
<BR><INPUT TYPE="radio" NAME="rating" VALUE="very good">Very Good
<BR><INPUT TYPE="radio" NAME="rating" VALUE="good">Good
<BR><INPUT TYPE="radio" NAME="rating" VALUE="poor">Poor</P>

<P>Suggestions/Comments:
<BR><TEXTAREA ></P>

<P><INPUT TYPE="submit" VALUE="Send">
<INPUT TYPE="reset" VALUE="Clear"></P>
</FORM>

</BODY>
</HTML>
```

1 Between the <FORM> and </FORM> tags, type the text you want to appear beside the large text area.

2 Type **<TEXTAREA** and then press the **Spacebar**.

Note: If you want the text area to appear on its own line, use the P or BR tag. For more information, see pages 36 and 38.

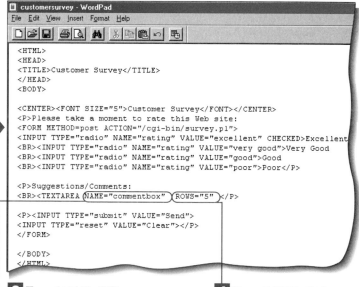

```
customersurvey - WordPad
File  Edit  View  Insert  Format  Help

<HTML>
<HEAD>
<TITLE>Customer Survey</TITLE>
</HEAD>
<BODY>

<CENTER><FONT SIZE="5">Customer Survey</FONT></CENTER>
<P>Please take a moment to rate this Web site:
<FORM METHOD=post ACTION="/cgi-bin/survey.pl">
<INPUT TYPE="radio" NAME="rating" VALUE="excellent" CHECKED>Excellent
<BR><INPUT TYPE="radio" NAME="rating" VALUE="very good">Very Good
<BR><INPUT TYPE="radio" NAME="rating" VALUE="good">Good
<BR><INPUT TYPE="radio" NAME="rating" VALUE="poor">Poor</P>

<P>Suggestions/Comments:
<BR><TEXTAREA NAME="commentbox" ROWS="5"></P>

<P><INPUT TYPE="submit" VALUE="Send">
<INPUT TYPE="reset" VALUE="Clear"></P>
</FORM>

</BODY>
</HTML>
```

3 Type **NAME="?"** replacing **?** with a word that describes the text area. Then press the **Spacebar**.

Note: The text you enter in step 3 identifies the text area to the Web server and will not appear on your Web page.

4 Type **ROWS="?"** replacing **?** with a height for the text area in rows. Then press the **Spacebar**.

How large should I make a text area?

You should make sure a text area will fit on a computer screen and will be wide enough to clearly display the text readers type. A text area with a height of approximately 15 rows and a width of approximately 70 characters will fill a computer screen.

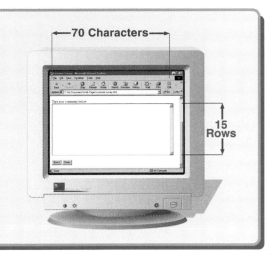

←— 70 Characters —→

15 Rows

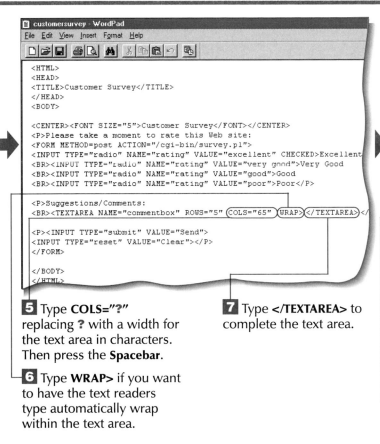

```
<HTML>
<HEAD>
<TITLE>Customer Survey</TITLE>
</HEAD>
<BODY>

<CENTER><FONT SIZE="5">Customer Survey</FONT></CENTER>
<P>Please take a moment to rate this Web site:
<FORM METHOD=post ACTION="/cgi-bin/survey.pl">
<INPUT TYPE="radio" NAME="rating" VALUE="excellent" CHECKED>Excellent
<BR><INPUT TYPE="radio" NAME="rating" VALUE="very good">Very Good
<BR><INPUT TYPE="radio" NAME="rating" VALUE="good">Good
<BR><INPUT TYPE="radio" NAME="rating" VALUE="poor">Poor</P>

<P>Suggestions/Comments:
<BR><TEXTAREA NAME="commentbox" ROWS="5" COLS="65" WRAP></TEXTAREA></

<P><INPUT TYPE="submit" VALUE="Send">
<INPUT TYPE="reset" VALUE="Clear"></P>
</FORM>

</BODY>
</HTML>
```

5 Type **COLS="?"** replacing **?** with a width for the text area in characters. Then press the **Spacebar**.

6 Type **WRAP>** if you want to have the text readers type automatically wrap within the text area.

7 Type **</TEXTAREA>** to complete the text area.

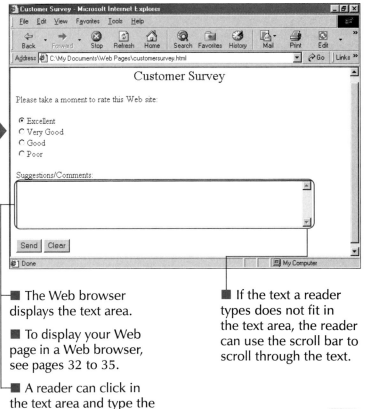

■ The Web browser displays the text area.

■ To display your Web page in a Web browser, see pages 32 to 35.

■ A reader can click in the text area and type the requested information.

■ If the text a reader types does not fit in the text area, the reader can use the scroll bar to scroll through the text.

CREATE CHECK BOXES

Which of the following states have you visited?

☑ California   ☑ Florida

☑ New York   ☐ Arizona

☐ Texas   ☑ Ohio

You can include check boxes on a form if you want readers to be able to select one or more options.

CREATE CHECK BOXES

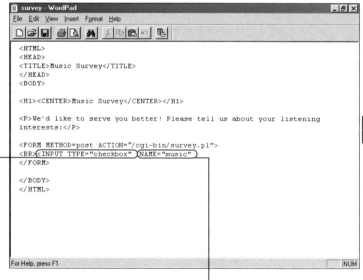

```
<HTML>
<HEAD>
<TITLE>Music Survey</TITLE>
</HEAD>
<BODY>

<H1><CENTER>Music Survey</CENTER></H1>

<P>We'd like to serve you better! Please tell us about your listening
interests:</P>

<FORM METHOD=post ACTION="/cgi-bin/survey.pl">
<BR><INPUT TYPE="checkbox" NAME="music"
</FORM>

</BODY>
</HTML>
```

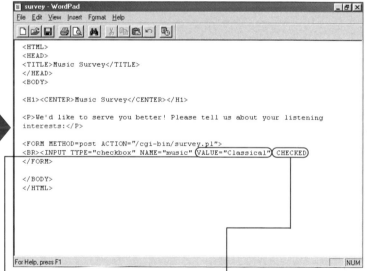

```
<HTML>
<HEAD>
<TITLE>Music Survey</TITLE>
</HEAD>
<BODY>

<H1><CENTER>Music Survey</CENTER></H1>

<P>We'd like to serve you better! Please tell us about your listening
interests:</P>

<FORM METHOD=post ACTION="/cgi-bin/survey.pl">
<BR><INPUT TYPE="checkbox" NAME="music" VALUE="Classical" CHECKED>
</FORM>

</BODY>
</HTML>
```

1 Between the <FORM> and </FORM> tags, type **<INPUT TYPE="checkbox"** and then press the **Spacebar**.

2 Type **NAME="?"** replacing **?** with a word that describes the group of check boxes you want to create. Then press the **Spacebar**.

Note: The text you enter in step **2** identifies the group of check boxes to the Web server and will not appear on your Web page.

3 To specify the information for one check box, type **VALUE="?"** replacing **?** with a word that describes the check box.

Note: The text you enter in step **3** identifies the check box to the Web server and will not appear on your Web page.

4 If you want the check box to be selected automatically, press the **Spacebar** and then type **CHECKED**.

134

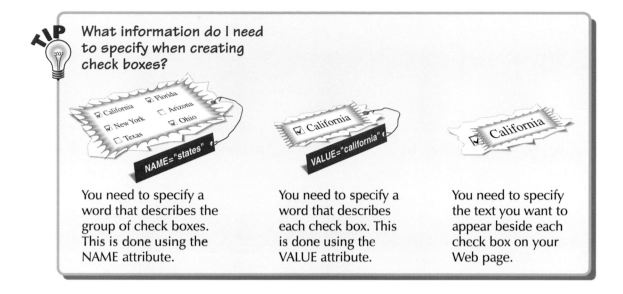

What information do I need to specify when creating check boxes?

You need to specify a word that describes the group of check boxes. This is done using the NAME attribute.

You need to specify a word that describes each check box. This is done using the VALUE attribute.

You need to specify the text you want to appear beside each check box on your Web page.

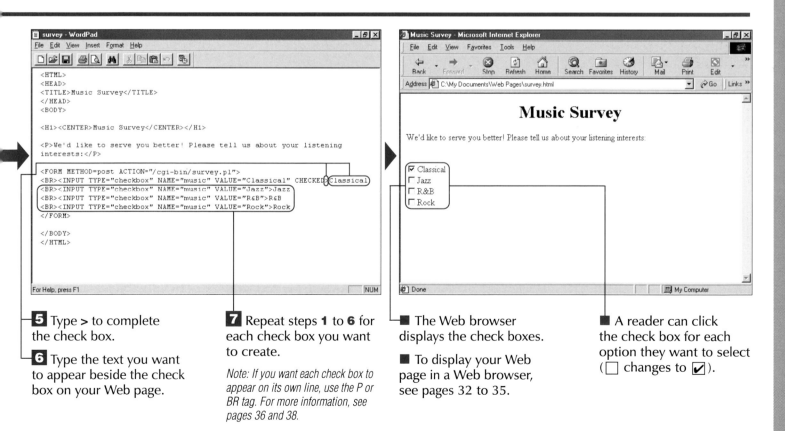

5 Type **>** to complete the check box.

6 Type the text you want to appear beside the check box on your Web page.

7 Repeat steps **1** to **6** for each check box you want to create.

Note: If you want each check box to appear on its own line, use the P or BR tag. For more information, see pages 36 and 38.

■ The Web browser displays the check boxes.

■ To display your Web page in a Web browser, see pages 32 to 35.

■ A reader can click the check box for each option they want to select (☐ changes to ☑).

You can include radio buttons on a form if you want readers to select only one of several options.

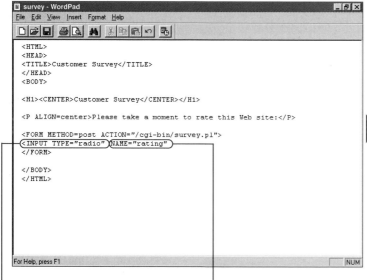

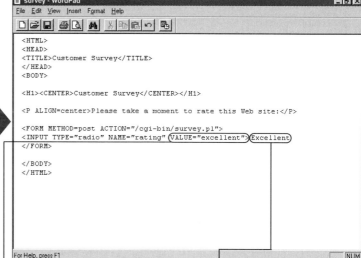

1 Between the <FORM> and </FORM> tags, type **<INPUT TYPE="radio"** and then press the **Spacebar**.

2 Type **NAME="?"** replacing **?** with a word that describes the group of radio buttons you want to create. Then press the **Spacebar**.

Note: The text you enter in step 2 identifies the group of radio buttons to the Web server and will not appear on your Web page.

3 To specify the information for one radio button, type **VALUE="?">** replacing **?** with a word that describes the radio button.

Note: The text you enter in step 3 identifies the radio button to the Web server and will not appear on your Web page.

4 Type the text you want to appear beside the radio button on your Web page.

TIP

What information do I need to specify when creating radio buttons?

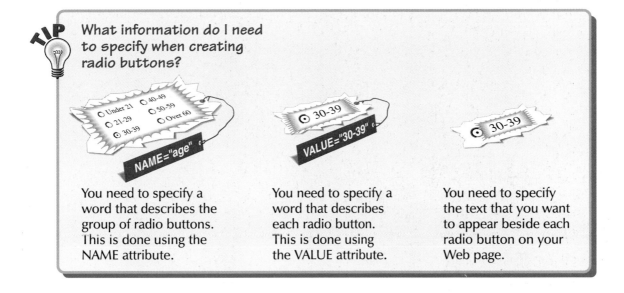

You need to specify a word that describes the group of radio buttons. This is done using the NAME attribute.

You need to specify a word that describes each radio button. This is done using the VALUE attribute.

You need to specify the text that you want to appear beside each radio button on your Web page.

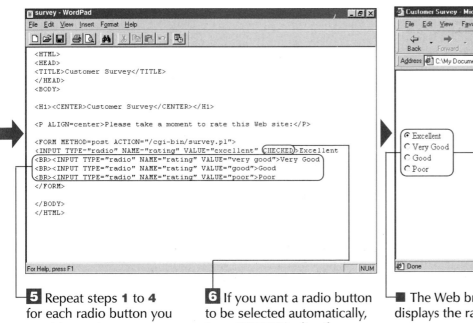

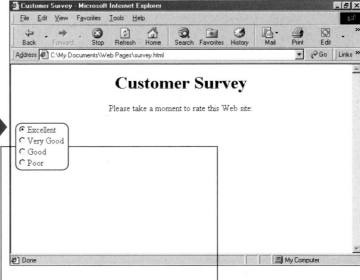

5 Repeat steps **1** to **4** for each radio button you want to create.

Note: If you want each radio button to appear on its own line, use the P or BR tag. For more information, see pages 36 and 38.

6 If you want a radio button to be selected automatically, type **CHECKED** after the VALUE attribute for the radio button.

Note: You can have only one radio button selected automatically.

■ The Web browser displays the radio buttons.

■ To display your Web page in a Web browser, see pages 32 to 35.

■ A reader can click a radio button to select one of several options (○ changes to ⊙).

CREATE A SUBMIT BUTTON

You can create a Submit button that readers can click to send the information they entered in your form to your Web server.

CREATE A SUBMIT BUTTON

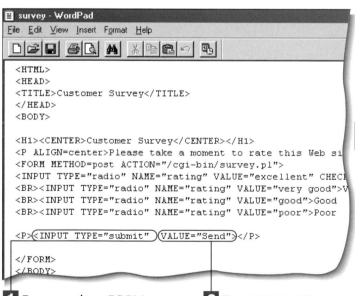

```
<HTML>
<HEAD>
<TITLE>Customer Survey</TITLE>
</HEAD>
<BODY>

<H1><CENTER>Customer Survey</CENTER></H1>
<P ALIGN=center>Please take a moment to rate this Web si
<FORM METHOD=post ACTION="/cgi-bin/survey.pl">
<INPUT TYPE="radio" NAME="rating" VALUE="excellent" CHEC
<BR><INPUT TYPE="radio" NAME="rating" VALUE="very good">V
<BR><INPUT TYPE="radio" NAME="rating" VALUE="good">Good
<BR><INPUT TYPE="radio" NAME="rating" VALUE="poor">Poor

<P><INPUT TYPE="submit" VALUE="Send"></P>

</FORM>
</BODY>
```

1 Between the <FORM> and </FORM> tags, type **<INPUT TYPE="submit"** and then press the **Spacebar**.

2 Type **VALUE="?">** replacing **?** with the text you want to appear on the Submit button.

Note: If you want the Submit button to appear on its own line, use the P or BR tag. For more information, see pages 36 and 38.

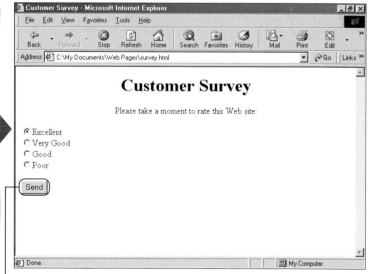

■ The Web browser displays the Submit button.

■ To display your Web page in a Web browser, see pages 32 to 35.

■ When a reader clicks the Submit button, the information they entered in your form will transfer to your Web server.

You can create a Reset button that readers can click to clear the information they entered in your form.

CREATE A RESET BUTTON

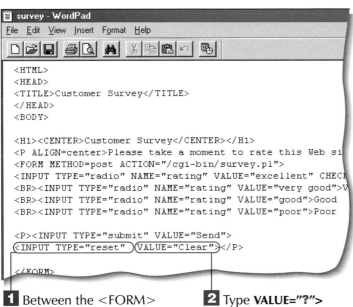

```
<HTML>
<HEAD>
<TITLE>Customer Survey</TITLE>
</HEAD>
<BODY>

<H1><CENTER>Customer Survey</CENTER></H1>
<P ALIGN=center>Please take a moment to rate this Web si
<FORM METHOD=post ACTION="/cgi-bin/survey.pl">
<INPUT TYPE="radio" NAME="rating" VALUE="excellent" CHEC
<BR><INPUT TYPE="radio" NAME="rating" VALUE="very good">V
<BR><INPUT TYPE="radio" NAME="rating" VALUE="good">Good
<BR><INPUT TYPE="radio" NAME="rating" VALUE="poor">Poor

<P><INPUT TYPE="submit" VALUE="Send">
<INPUT TYPE="reset" VALUE="Clear"></P>

</FORM>
```

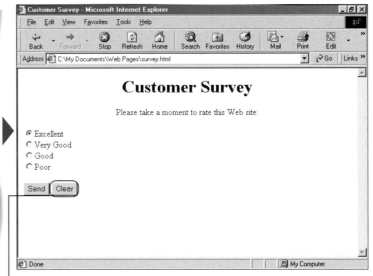

1 Between the <FORM> and </FORM> tags, type **<INPUT TYPE="reset"** and then press the **Spacebar**.

2 Type **VALUE="?">** replacing **?** with the text you want to appear on the Reset button.

Note: If you want the Reset button to appear on its own line, use the P or BR tag. For more information, see pages 36 and 38.

■ The Web browser displays the Reset button.

■ To display your Web page in a Web browser, see pages 32 to 35.

■ When a reader clicks the Reset button, the form clears and once again displays its original settings.

ADVANCED WEB PAGES

Would you like to make your Web pages more impressive and exciting? This chapter will show you how to add sounds and videos, create an image map and much more.

ADD SOUNDS

REASONS FOR ADDING SOUNDS

ENTERTAINMENT

Entertainment is the most popular reason for including sounds on Web pages. You can include sound clips from television shows, movies, famous speeches and theme songs.

SALES

Adding sounds to Web pages is useful if you sell products such as music CDs or audio tapes. People may be more likely to buy a product if they can listen to a sample of the product first.

TYPES OF SOUNDS

You can include several types of sounds on a Web page. The most popular type of sound is WAVE. You can determine the type of a sound by the characters that appear after the period in the sound file name (example: birdchirp.wav).

Type of Sound	Extension	Used For
MIDI	.mid	Instrumental music
MPEG	.mp3	Songs
RealAudio	.ra	Live broadcasts
WAVE	.wav	Short sound clips

WHERE TO GET SOUNDS

THE INTERNET

There are many places on the Internet that offer sounds you can use for free on your Web pages. Make sure you have permission to use any sounds you obtain on the Internet.

You can find sounds at the following Web sites:

earthstation1.com

soundamerica.com

wavcentral.com

COMPUTER STORES

Many computer stores offer collections of sounds that you can purchase. Sound collections can include theme songs, nature sounds and special effects. Make sure sounds you purchase are in a format commonly used on the Web, such as WAVE.

RECORD SOUNDS

If your computer has sound capabilities, you can use a sound recording program to record sounds. You can connect a microphone to your computer to record your own voice or connect a CD or cassette player to record music or other sounds. When recording a sound you did not create, make sure you have permission to use the sound on your Web page.

Windows includes a sound recording program called Sound Recorder. The latest Macintosh computers include a sound recording program called QuickTime that you can also obtain at the www.apple.com/quicktime Web site.

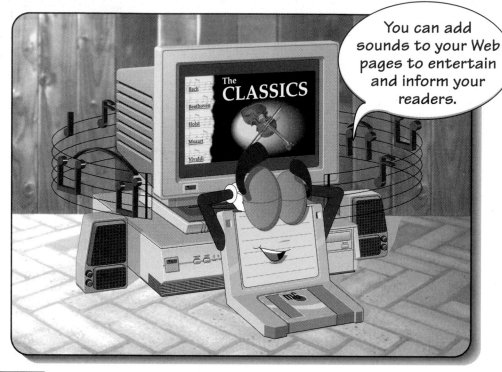

You can add sounds to your Web pages to entertain and inform your readers.

Make sure the sounds you add are in a format commonly used on the Web. For information on the types of sounds, see page 142.

Whenever possible, you should use small sound files. Large sound files can take a long time to transfer to a computer.

ADD A SOUND

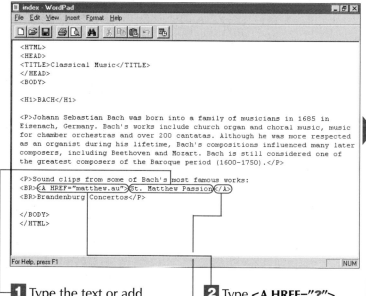

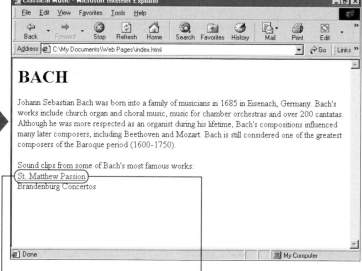

1 Type the text or add the image you want readers to select to play the sound. To add an image, see page 70.

2 Type **<A HREF="?">** in front of the text or image, replacing **?** with the location of the sound on your computer.

Note: For information on specifying the location of a sound, see page 145.

3 Type **</A>** after the text or image.

■ The Web browser displays the sound link on your Web page.

■ To display your Web page in a Web browser, see pages 32 to 35.

■ When a reader selects the sound link, the sound will transfer to their computer and play.

SOUND CONSIDERATIONS

PROVIDE DESCRIPTIONS

You should provide a short description of a sound you add to a Web page. Include the sound type, size and length of time the sound will play. Readers can use this information to decide if they want to play the sound.

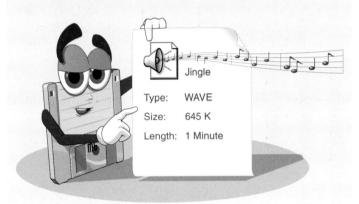

SOUND ALTERNATIVES

Some readers may be hearing impaired or use computers that cannot play sounds. Other readers may not be able to play certain types of sounds. You should consider including a text version of important sounds on your Web page.

SPECIFY LOCATION OF SOUNDS

You should store all of your sounds and Web pages in one folder on your computer. If the folder contains many files, you may want to store your sounds in a subfolder.

If a sound you want to add to a Web page is stored in the same folder as the Web page, you can specify just the name of the sound (example: birdchirp.wav).

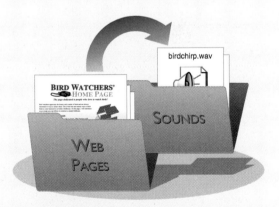

If a sound is stored in a subfolder, you must specify the name of the subfolder and the name of the sound (example: sounds/birdchirp.wav).

REASONS FOR ADDING VIDEOS

ENTERTAINMENT

Videos can entertain readers who visit your Web pages. You can include videos to present eye-catching visual effects, movie clips, animation or home videos.

PROVIDE INFORMATION

You can include videos on your Web pages to provide information about a company, organization or topic of interest. A video can show a TV broadcast, interview, press announcement or a demonstration of a product or service.

TYPES OF VIDEOS

You can include several types of videos on a Web page. You can determine the type of a video by the characters that appear after the period in the video file name (example: plane.avi). Some Web browsers can play only certain types of video, while other Web browsers cannot play any video types.

Type of Video	Extension
AVI	.avi
MPEG	.mpg or .mpeg
QuickTime	.mov

WHERE TO GET VIDEOS

THE INTERNET

There are many places on the Internet that offer videos you can use for free on your Web pages. Make sure you have permission to use any videos you obtain on the Internet.

You can find videos at the following Web sites:

moviecentral.hypermart.net

www.jurassicpunk.com

www.nasa.gov/gallery/video

COMPUTER STORES

Many computer stores offer collections of videos that you can purchase. Video collections can include movie clips, special effects and nature clips. Make sure videos you purchase are in a format commonly used on the Web, such as AVI.

RECORD VIDEOS

If your computer has a video capture card, you can connect a VCR, video camera or DVD player to your computer to record videos. Video capture cards usually include all the necessary cables and software you need to record videos. When recording a video you did not create, make sure you have permission to use the video on your Web page.

You can add an external video to your Web page. An external video will play when readers select a link on your Web page.

Make sure the video you add is in a format commonly used on the Web. For information on the types of videos, see page 146.

ADD AN EXTERNAL VIDEO

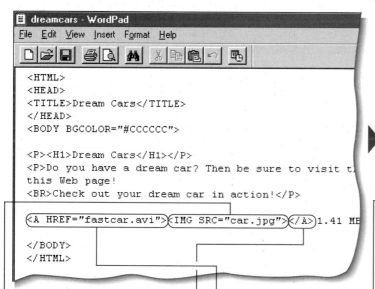

```
<HTML>
<HEAD>
<TITLE>Dream Cars</TITLE>
</HEAD>
<BODY BGCOLOR="#CCCCCC">

<P><H1>Dream Cars</H1></P>
<P>Do you have a dream car? Then be sure to visit t
this Web page!
<BR>Check out your dream car in action!</P>

<A HREF="fastcar.avi"><IMG SRC="car.jpg"></A>1.41 ME

</BODY>
</HTML>
```

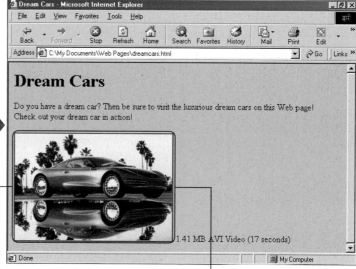

1 Type the text or add the image you want readers to select to play the video. To add an image, see page 70.

2 Type **<A HREF="?">** in front of the text or image, replacing **?** with the location of the video on your computer.

Note: For information on specifying the location of a video, see page 149.

3 Type **</A>** after the text or image.

■ The Web browser displays the video link on your Web page.

■ To display your Web page in a Web browser, see pages 32 to 35.

■ When a reader selects the video link, the video will transfer to their computer and play.

VIDEO CONSIDERATIONS

USE SMALL VIDEO FILES

Video files tend to be the largest files on the Web. Videos with large file sizes can take a long time to transfer to a computer. Whenever possible, you should use videos with small file sizes.

PROVIDE DESCRIPTIONS

Provide a short description of a video you add to your Web page, including the type, size and length of time the video will play. Readers can use this information to decide if they want to play the video.

Skiing in Colorado

Type: MPEG

Size: 800 K

Length: 35 sec.

SPECIFY LOCATION OF VIDEOS

You should store all of your videos and Web pages in one folder on your computer. If the folder contains many files, you may want to store your videos in a subfolder.

page1.html

index.html

airplane.avi

WEB PAGES and VIDEOS

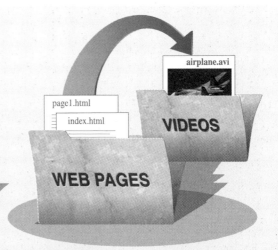

airplane.avi

page1.html

index.html

VIDEOS

WEB PAGES

If a video you want to add to a Web page is stored in the same folder as the Web page, you can specify just the name of the video (example: airplane.avi).

If a video is stored in a subfolder, you must specify the name of the subfolder and the name of the video (example: videos/airplane.avi).

You can add an internal video to your Web page. An internal video will play directly on the Web page.

When adding an internal video, you should only use AVI videos. For information on the types of videos, see page 146.

ADD AN INTERNAL VIDEO

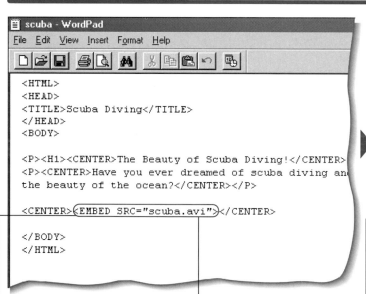

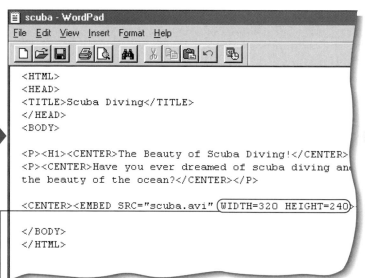

1 Position the cursor where you want the video to appear on your Web page.

2 Type **<EMBED SRC="?">** replacing **?** with the location of the video on your computer.

Note: For information on specifying the location of a video, see page 149.

3 In the <EMBED> tag, type **WIDTH=? HEIGHT=?** replacing **?** with the width and height of the video in pixels.

Note: For more information, see the top of page 151.

What width and height should I specify for my video?

You can use a video player to determine the correct width and height of a video. You should specify the correct dimensions for a video to make sure the video appears correctly in a Web browser. Windows comes with a video player called Windows Media Player. You can also use the QuickTime video player that you can obtain at the www.apple.com/quicktime Web site.

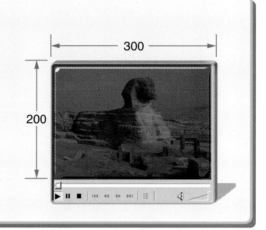

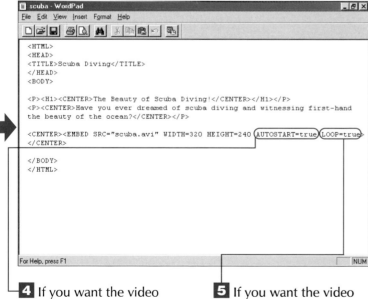

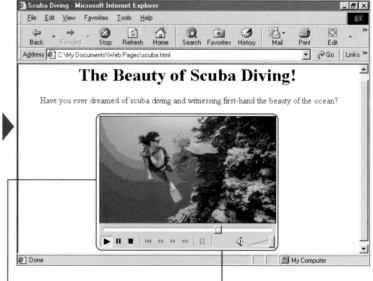

4 If you want the video to play automatically when a reader visits your Web page, type **AUTOSTART=true** in the <EMBED> tag.

5 If you want the video to play continuously until a reader clicks the video or displays another Web page, type **LOOP=true** in the <EMBED> tag.

■ The Web browser displays the video on your Web page.

■ To display your Web page in a Web browser, see pages 32 to 35.

■ A reader can click the video to start or stop the video at any time.

REASONS FOR ADDING JAVA APPLETS

ENTERTAINMENT

Java applets can make your Web pages more entertaining by adding special effects such as rotating images, fireworks and animated text. Java applets can also allow readers to play simple games and chat with other people viewing your Web pages.

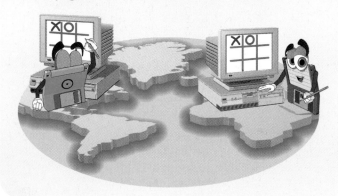

PROVIDE INFORMATION

Java applets are ideal for displaying information that constantly changes, such as stock market updates, the time, weather information and news headlines. Java applets can also perform complex calculations such as calculating a mortgage.

WHERE TO GET JAVA APPLETS

THE INTERNET

There are many places on the Internet that offer Java applets you can use for free on your Web pages. Most Java applets come with instructions on how to properly add the applets to a Web page. You can find Java applets at the following Web sites:

javaboutique.internet.com

www.javashareware.com

www.gamelan.com

CREATE JAVA APPLETS

If you know the Java programming language, you can create your own Java applets that you can add to your Web pages. You can learn about the Java programming language at the java.sun.com Web site.

JAVA APPLET CONSIDERATIONS

INCREASE TRANSFER TIME

Java applets can significantly increase the time it takes for a Web page to transfer over the Internet and appear on a screen. If a Web page takes too long to appear, readers may lose interest and move to another Web page.

JAVA APPLETS MAY NOT APPEAR

The Java applets on your Web pages may not appear for some readers. Some readers may use older Web browsers that cannot run Java applets, while others may turn off Java applets in their Web browsers.

ADD JAVA APPLETS

You can add Java applets to your Web pages to entertain and inform your readers.

Java applets have the .class extension (example: fireworks.class).

ADD A JAVA APPLET

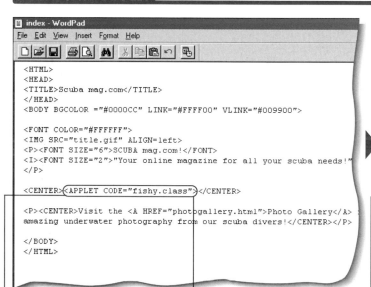

```
index - WordPad
File  Edit  View  Insert  Format  Help

<HTML>
<HEAD>
<TITLE>Scuba mag.com</TITLE>
</HEAD>
<BODY BGCOLOR ="#0000CC" LINK="#FFFF00" VLINK="#009900">

<FONT COLOR="#FFFFFF">
<IMG SRC="title.gif" ALIGN=left>
<P><FONT SIZE="6">SCUBA mag.com!</FONT>
<I><FONT SIZE="2">"Your online magazine for all your scuba needs!"
</P>

<CENTER><APPLET CODE="fishy.class"></CENTER>

<P><CENTER>Visit the <A HREF="photogallery.html">Photo Gallery</A>
amazing underwater photography from our scuba divers!</CENTER></P>

</BODY>
</HTML>
```

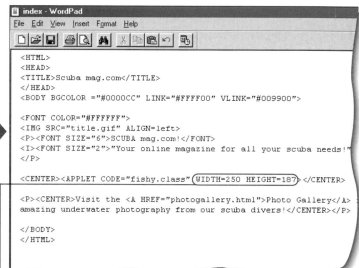

```
index - WordPad
File  Edit  View  Insert  Format  Help

<HTML>
<HEAD>
<TITLE>Scuba mag.com</TITLE>
</HEAD>
<BODY BGCOLOR ="#0000CC" LINK="#FFFF00" VLINK="#009900">

<FONT COLOR="#FFFFFF">
<IMG SRC="title.gif" ALIGN=left>
<P><FONT SIZE="6">SCUBA mag.com!</FONT>
<I><FONT SIZE="2">"Your online magazine for all your scuba needs!"
</P>

<CENTER><APPLET CODE="fishy.class" WIDTH=250 HEIGHT=187></CENTER>

<P><CENTER>Visit the <A HREF="photogallery.html">Photo Gallery</A>
amazing underwater photography from our scuba divers!</CENTER></P>

</BODY>
</HTML>
```

1 Position the cursor where you want the Java applet to appear on your Web page.

2 Type **<APPLET CODE="?">** replacing **?** with the location of the Java applet on your computer.

Note: You can specify the location of a Java applet as you would specify the location of an image. For more information, see page 71.

3 In the <APPLET> tag, type **WIDTH=? HEIGHT=?** replacing **?** with the width and height of the Java applet in pixels.

Note: For information on specifying the width and height of a Java applet, see the top of page 155.

What width and height should I specify for a Java applet?

If you obtained a Java applet on the Internet, the applet will usually come with instructions that indicate the correct width and height of the applet. If you do not specify the correct width and height of a Java applet, all or part of the applet may not appear on your Web page.

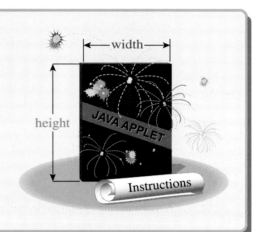

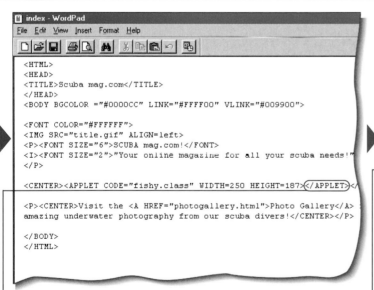

4 Type **</APPLET>** to complete the Java applet.

■ The Web browser runs the Java applet on your Web page.

■ To display your Web page in a Web browser, see pages 32 to 35.

ADD JAVASCRIPT

JavaScript can make your Web pages interactive and entertaining.

JavaScript can display alert messages, offer drop down menus, open new windows and change images in response to mouse movements. Although the names are similar, JavaScript and Java have very little in common.

WHERE TO GET JAVASCRIPT

THE INTERNET

There are many places on the Internet that offer JavaScripts you can use for free on your Web pages. Make sure you have permission to use any JavaScripts you obtain on the Internet. Most JavaScripts come with instructions on how to properly add the JavaScript to a Web page. You can find JavaScripts at the following Web sites:

javascript.internet.com

www.javagoodies.com

www.javascripts.com

CREATE JAVASCRIPTS

If you know the JavaScript scripting language, you can create your own JavaScripts that you can add to your Web pages. You can learn about the JavaScript scripting language at the www.htmlgoodies.com/primers/jsp Web site.

You can add JavaScript to make your Web pages dynamic and interactive.

ADD JAVASCRIPT

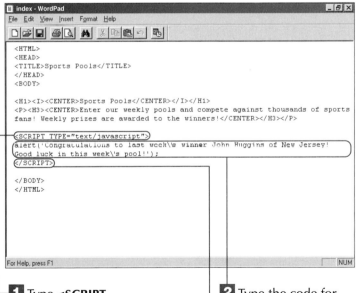

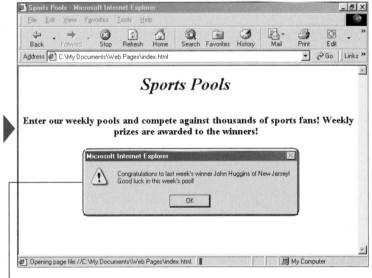

1 Type **<SCRIPT TYPE="text/javascript">** on your Web page.

Note: To determine where to place the JavaScript on your Web page, check the instructions included with the JavaScript.

2 Type the code for the JavaScript.

Note: For information on where you can get JavaScripts, see page 156.

3 Type **</SCRIPT>**.

■ The Web browser runs the JavaScript on your Web page.

■ To display your Web page in a Web browser, see pages 32 to 35.

ADD JAVASCRIPT

You can hide JavaScript from older Web browsers that cannot understand JavaScript.

If you do not hide JavaScript from older Web browsers, the Web browsers may display the code for the JavaScript on your Web page.

HIDE JAVASCRIPT

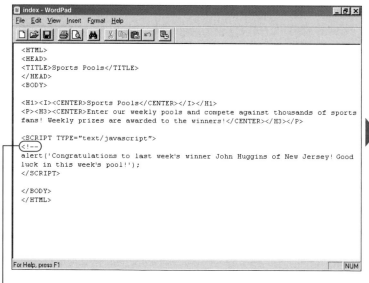

```
<HTML>
<HEAD>
<TITLE>Sports Pools</TITLE>
</HEAD>
<BODY>

<H1><I><CENTER>Sports Pools</CENTER></I></H1>
<P><H3><CENTER>Enter our weekly pools and compete against thousands of sports
fans! Weekly prizes are awarded to the winners!</CENTER></H3></P>

<SCRIPT TYPE="text/javascript">
<!--
alert('Congratulations to last week's winner John Huggins of New Jersey! Good
luck in this week's pool!');
</SCRIPT>

</BODY>
</HTML>
```

1 Type **<!--** directly below the <SCRIPT> tag.

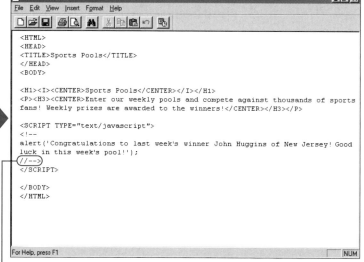

```
<HTML>
<HEAD>
<TITLE>Sports Pools</TITLE>
</HEAD>
<BODY>

<H1><I><CENTER>Sports Pools</CENTER></I></H1>
<P><H3><CENTER>Enter our weekly pools and compete against thousands of sports
fans! Weekly prizes are awarded to the winners!</CENTER></H3></P>

<SCRIPT TYPE="text/javascript">
<!--
alert('Congratulations to last week's winner John Huggins of New Jersey! Good
luck in this week's pool!');
//-->
</SCRIPT>

</BODY>
</HTML>
```

2 Type **//-->** directly above the </SCRIPT> tag.

■ If a reader displays your Web page in an older Web browser that cannot run JavaScript, the JavaScript code will not appear.

You can provide text that you want to display if a Web browser does not run JavaScript. This will tell readers what they are missing.

Some readers use old Web browsers that cannot run JavaScript, while others may turn off JavaScript in their Web browsers.

PROVIDE ALTERNATIVE TEXT

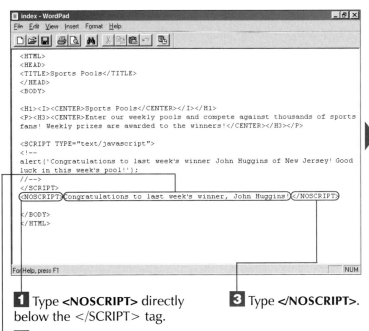

1 Type **<NOSCRIPT>** directly below the </SCRIPT> tag.

2 Type the text you want to display if a Web browser does not run JavaScript.

3 Type **</NOSCRIPT>**.

■ If JavaScript does not run, the Web browser will display the text you specified.

■ To display your Web page in a Web browser, see pages 32 to 35.

You can create an image map that divides an image into different areas that each link to a different Web page.

When creating an image map, you should use an image that has several distinct areas that readers can select. Photographs do not usually make good image maps.

CREATE AN IMAGE MAP

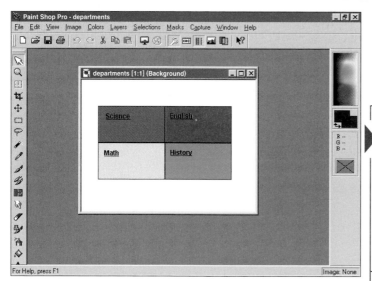

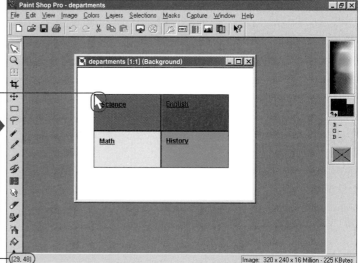

DETERMINE COORDINATES OF IMAGE AREAS

To determine the coordinates of each image area, you need an image editing program such as Paint Shop Pro. You can obtain Paint Shop Pro at computer stores or at the www.jasc.com Web site.

1 Start your image editing program. In this example, we started Paint Shop Pro.

2 Open the image you want to use as an image map.

3 Position the mouse ⬚ over a point on the image for the coordinates you need. For more information, see the top of page 161.

4 Write down the coordinates displayed in this area.

5 Repeat steps **3** and **4** until you have all the coordinates for the image area.

6 Repeat steps **3** to **5** until you have all the coordinates for each image area.

TIP

What coordinates do I need for each area in an image map?

The coordinates you need depend on the shape of each area.

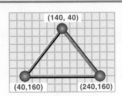

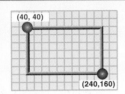

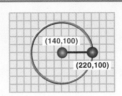

Rectangle
- Top left corner
- Bottom right corner

Polygon (Irregular Shape)
- Each point on the polygon

Circle
- Center of circle
- Right edge of circle

Note: You need the coordinates of the right edge of the circle to calculate the radius of the circle. To calculate the radius, subtract the first coordinate for the center of the circle (140) from the first coordinate for the right edge of the circle (220).

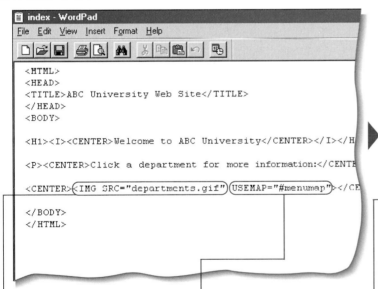

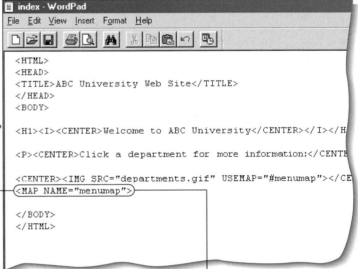

CREATE AN IMAGE MAP

1 Add the image you want to use as an image map to your Web page. To add an image, see page 70.

2 In the <IMG> tag for the image, type **USEMAP="#?"** replacing **?** with a name for the image map.

3 Position the cursor where you want to enter the information for the image map. Most people enter this information at the bottom of the Web page.

4 Type **<MAP NAME="?">** replacing **?** with the image map name you typed in step **2**.

CONTINUED

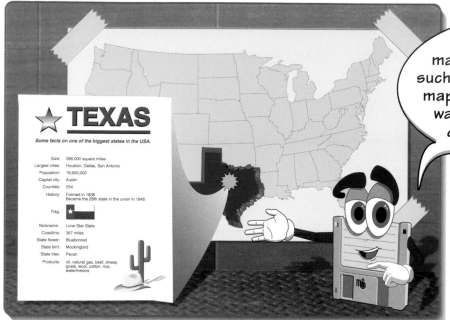

Creating an image map is useful for images such as a floor plan, campus map or world map that you want to contain links to different Web pages.

CREATE AN IMAGE MAP (CONTINUED)

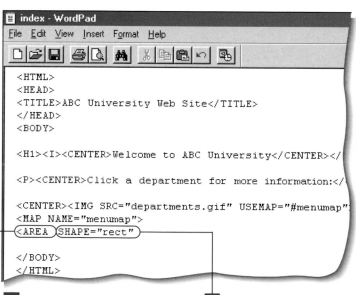

```
index - WordPad
File  Edit  View  Insert  Format  Help

<HTML>
<HEAD>
<TITLE>ABC University Web Site</TITLE>
</HEAD>
<BODY>

<H1><I><CENTER>Welcome to ABC University</CENTER></

<P><CENTER>Click a department for more information:</

<CENTER><IMG SRC="departments.gif" USEMAP="#menumap"
<MAP NAME="menumap">
<AREA SHAPE="rect"

</BODY>
</HTML>
```

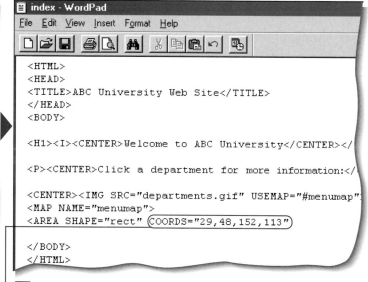

```
index - WordPad
File  Edit  View  Insert  Format  Help

<HTML>
<HEAD>
<TITLE>ABC University Web Site</TITLE>
</HEAD>
<BODY>

<H1><I><CENTER>Welcome to ABC University</CENTER></

<P><CENTER>Click a department for more information:</

<CENTER><IMG SRC="departments.gif" USEMAP="#menumap"
<MAP NAME="menumap">
<AREA SHAPE="rect" COORDS="29,48,152,113"

</BODY>
</HTML>
```

5 Type **<AREA** to specify the information for one image area of the image map. Then press the **Spacebar**.

6 Type **SHAPE="?"** replacing **?** with the shape of the area (**rect** for rectangle, **circle** for circle or **poly** for an irregular shape). Then press the **Spacebar**.

7 For a rectangle, type **COORDS="a,b,c,d"** where **a,b** are the coordinates of the top left corner and **c,d** are the coordinates of the bottom right corner.

■ For a circle, type **COORDS="a,b,r"** where **a,b** are the coordinates for the center of the circle and **r** is the radius.

■ For a polygon, type **COORDS="a,b,c,d..."** where **a,b,c,d** and so on are the coordinates of each point on the polygon.

8 Press the **Spacebar**.

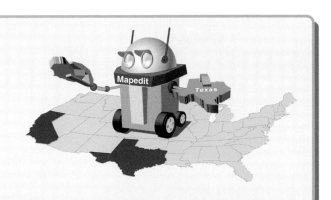

TIP

Is there an easier way to create an image map?

You can use the Mapedit program to help you create image maps. You can obtain Mapedit at the www.boutell.com/mapedit Web site.

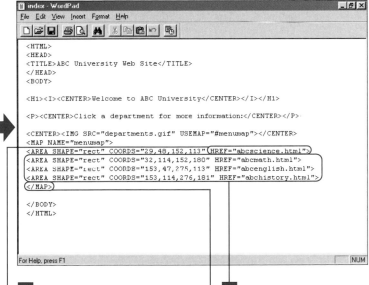

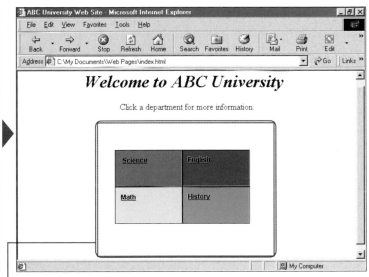

9 Type **HREF="?">** replacing **?** with the address of the Web page you want the image area to link to.

*Note: To link the image area to a Web page in your own Web site, replace **?** with the location of the Web page on your computer. For more information, see the top of page 103.*

10 Repeat steps **5** to **9** for each image area.

11 Type **</MAP>** to complete the image map.

■ The Web browser displays the image map on your Web page.

■ To display your Web page in a Web browser, see pages 32 to 35.

■ A reader can click an area of the image map to display the linked Web page.

CREATE FRAMES

You can create frames to divide a Web browser window into sections. Each section will display a different Web page.

REASONS FOR USING FRAMES

BANNERS

Frames allow you to display a banner that will remain on the screen while readers browse through your Web pages. Banners are useful for displaying information such as an advertisement, a warning message or a company logo.

NAVIGATION

You can place a table of contents, navigational tools or search tools in a frame to keep the information on the screen at all times. This information will help readers move through your Web pages and find information of interest.

SUPPORTING INFORMATION

You can use frames to display supporting information on the screen while readers move through your Web pages. This is ideal for information such as copyright notices, footnotes, references and other information related to your Web pages.

Copyright © 1999 Travel the World. All rights reserved.

CREATING FRAMES

STEP 1–CREATE WEB PAGES FOR FRAMES

You must create the Web pages you want to appear in the frames. Each frame will display a different Web page.

STEP 2–SET UP FRAMES

You must create a Web page that defines the structure of your frames. The page will contain information such as the number of frames you want to create and which Web page will appear in each frame. The page will not contain any information that readers will see.

FRAME CONSIDERATIONS

USING FRAMES

Try not to use too many frames since this can display too much information at once. Using too many frames can also make your Web pages difficult to read by reducing the amount of information each Web page can display.

SCREEN RESOLUTION

The resolution of a monitor determines the amount of information that will appear on a screen. When creating frames, you should make sure your Web pages appear the way you want on computers using different resolutions. Computers using lower resolutions will show less information in each frame.

You can create frames that divide a Web browser window into rows or columns.

Rows

Columns

CREATE FRAMES

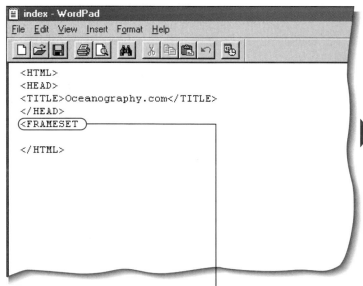

```
index - WordPad
File  Edit  View  Insert  Format  Help

<HTML>
<HEAD>
<TITLE>Oceanography.com</TITLE>
</HEAD>
<FRAMESET

</HTML>
```

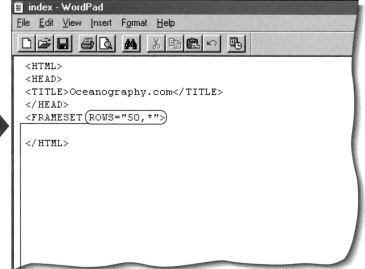

```
index - WordPad
File  Edit  View  Insert  Format  Help

<HTML>
<HEAD>
<TITLE>Oceanography.com</TITLE>
</HEAD>
<FRAMESET ROWS="50,*">

</HTML>
```

1 Set up a Web page as shown on pages 28 to 31. Do not type any text for the Web page or include the BODY tags.

2 Type **<FRAMESET** directly below the </HEAD> tag. Then press the **Spacebar**.

3 To create frames in rows, type **ROWS="a,b...">** replacing **a,b** and so on with the height of each row you want to create.

■ To create frames in columns, type **COLS="a,b...">** replacing **a,b** and so on with the width of each column you want to create.

Note: To specify the height or width of a frame, see the top of page 167.

How do I specify the height or width of a frame?

You can specify the height or width of a frame by typing a percentage of the window (example: 50%), a number of pixels (example: 300) or an asterisk (*). When you type an asterisk (*), the size of the frame will depend on the size of your other frames. For example, if one frame uses 70% of the window, the frame with the asterisk will use 30% of the window.

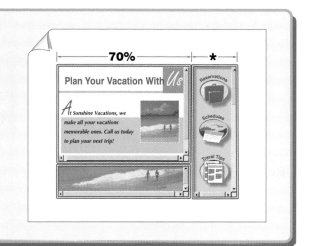

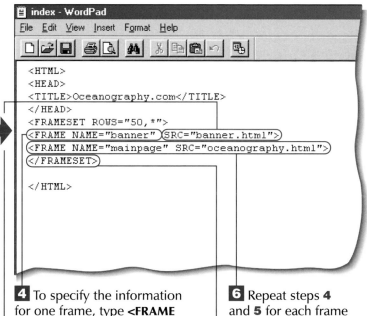

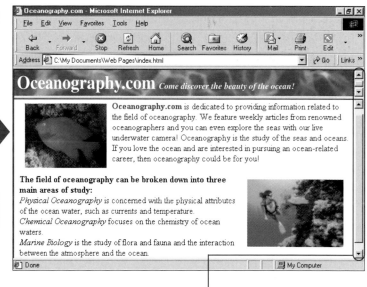

4 To specify the information for one frame, type **<FRAME NAME="?"** replacing **?** with a name for the frame. Then press the **Spacebar**.

5 Type **SRC="?">** replacing **?** with the location of the Web page you want to appear in the frame.

Note: To specify the location of a Web page in your own Web site, see the top of page 103.

6 Repeat steps **4** and **5** for each frame you created in step **3**.

7 Type **</FRAMESET>**.

■ The Web browser displays the frames.

■ To display your Web page in a Web browser, see pages 32 to 35.

■ Scroll bars appear automatically when a frame is too small to display the contents of an entire Web page. Readers can use the scroll bars to move through the Web page.

CREATE A LINK TO A FRAME

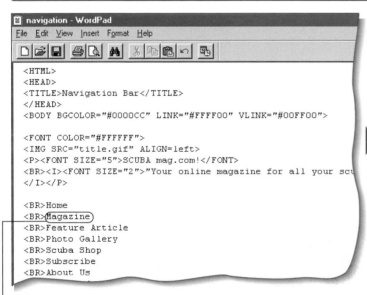

1 On the Web page you want to display the link, type the text or add the image you want readers to select to display a Web page in another frame. To add an image, see page 70.

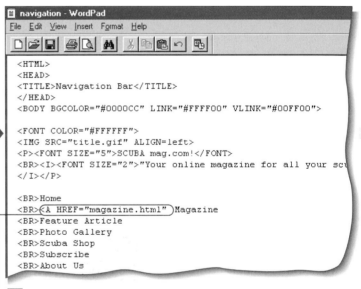

2 Type **<A HREF="?"** in front of the text or image, replacing **?** with the location of the Web page you want to appear in another frame. Then press the **Spacebar**.

Note: To specify the location of a Web page in your own Web site, see the top of page 103.

Can I create a link that opens a Web page in its own window?

If a Web page does not display well in a frame, you can create a link that will open the Web page in its own window.

New Window

To open a Web page in a new window, type **TARGET=_blank>** in step **3** below.

Current Window

To open a Web page in the current window, type **TARGET=_top>** in step **3** below.

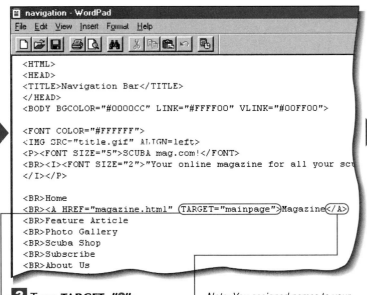

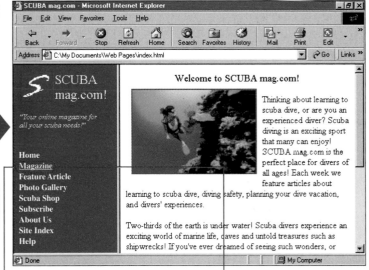

3 Type **TARGET="?">** replacing **?** with the name of the frame where you want the Web page to appear.

Note: You assigned names to your frames in step 4 on page 167.

4 Type **</A>** after the text or image.

■ The Web browser displays the link.

■ To display your Web page in a Web browser, see pages 32 to 35.

■ A reader can click the link to display the Web page in the frame you specified.

CHAPTER 11

USING STYLE SHEETS

Are you interested in learning how to format and lay out your Web pages using style sheets? This chapter will explain how to use style sheets to create impressive Web pages.

Arial, Blue

The land down under is the perfect winter getaway. Relaxing on the beach or exploring Australia's outback is an unforgettable experience!

Egypt

Discover Egypt's rich history and visit ancient marvels such

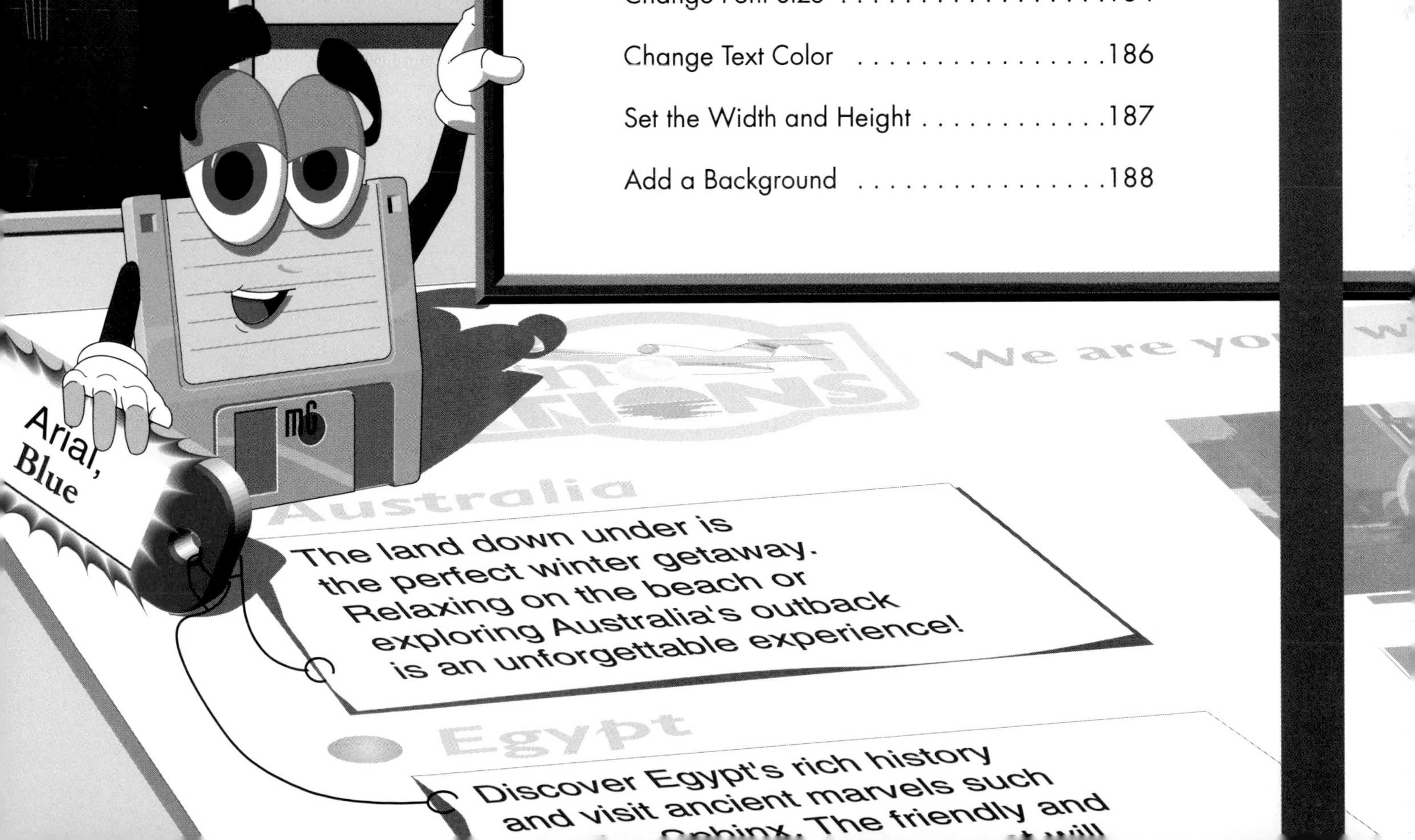

You can use style sheets to define the formatting and layout of information on your Web pages.

Style sheets are also known as Cascading Style Sheets (CSS). You can find more information about style sheets at the www.w3.org Web site.

HOW STYLE SHEETS WORK

A style sheet allows you to specify in one centralized location how you want information for each tag to appear on one or more Web pages. For example, you can specify that you want all H1 headings to appear in a specific font and color.

A style sheet allows you to perform the same tasks as many HTML tags and is now the preferred method for performing these tasks.

STYLE SHEET STRUCTURE

When creating a style sheet, you enter a tag you want to define characteristics for, such as H1 (H1 headings), P (paragraphs) or B (bold text) and then list the characteristics you want the tag to use. A semi-colon (;) must separate each characteristic. The characteristics you define for a tag will affect all the information that uses the tag on your Web page(s).

REASONS FOR USING STYLE SHEETS

ADDITIONAL FEATURES

Style sheets allow you to format and lay out text and images in ways you cannot accomplish with HTML tags. You can create sophisticated Web pages that look like pages from a magazine. For example, you can change the line spacing and specify the position of text and images on a Web page.

SAVE TIME

Style sheets allow you to define in one location how you want information that uses a tag to appear throughout your Web page(s). This saves you time since you do not have to type the same information in each individual tag. For example, you can define how you want all the text that uses the P (paragraph) tag to appear throughout a Web page.

EASY TO UPDATE

When you use style sheets, you can make changes to your Web page(s) in one centralized location. This prevents you from having to change each tag on your Web page(s) individually and helps maintain a consistent appearance for your Web page(s). For example, you can change the appearance of all your H1 headings at once.

SET UP A STYLE SHEET

You can set up a style sheet that will define the formatting and layout for a single Web page or multiple Web pages.

Single Web Page   **Multiple Web Pages**

FOR A SINGLE WEB PAGE

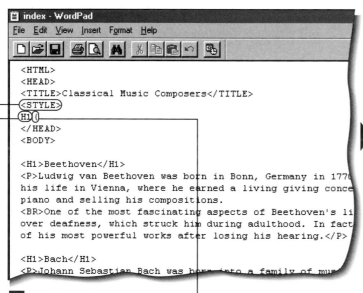

```
<HTML>
<HEAD>
<TITLE>Classical Music Composers</TITLE>
<STYLE>
H1{
</HEAD>
<BODY>

<H1>Beethoven</H1>
<P>Ludwig van Beethoven was born in Bonn, Germany in 1770
his life in Vienna, where he earned a living giving conce
piano and selling his compositions.
<BR>One of the most fascinating aspects of Beethoven's li
over deafness, which struck him during adulthood. In fact
of his most powerful works after losing his hearing.</P>

<H1>Bach</H1>
<P>Johann Sebastian Bach was born into a family of mus
```

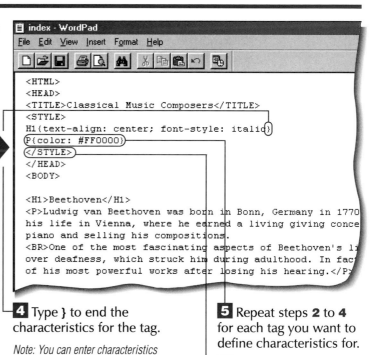

```
<HTML>
<HEAD>
<TITLE>Classical Music Composers</TITLE>
<STYLE>
H1{text-align: center; font-style: italic}
P{color: #FF0000}
</STYLE>
</HEAD>
<BODY>

<H1>Beethoven</H1>
<P>Ludwig van Beethoven was born in Bonn, Germany in 1770
his life in Vienna, where he earned a living giving conce
piano and selling his compositions.
<BR>One of the most fascinating aspects of Beethoven's li
over deafness, which struck him during adulthood. In fact
of his most powerful works after losing his hearing.</P>
```

1 On the Web page you want to use a style sheet, type **<STYLE>** between the <HEAD> and </HEAD> tags.

2 Type a tag you want to define characteristics for.

Note: You can define characteristics for tags such as H1 (H1 headings), P (paragraphs) and B (bold text).

3 Type **{** to begin the characteristics for the tag.

4 Type **}** to end the characteristics for the tag.

Note: You can enter characteristics for the tag between the brackets { }. A semi-colon (;) must separate each characteristic. To add characteristics, see pages 179 to 189.

5 Repeat steps **2** to **4** for each tag you want to define characteristics for.

6 Type **</STYLE>** to complete the style sheet.

TIP

When should I set up a style sheet for multiple Web pages?

Setting up a style sheet for multiple Web pages allows you to give all of your Web pages a consistent appearance. When you make changes to the style sheet, all the Web pages that use the style sheet will display the changes.

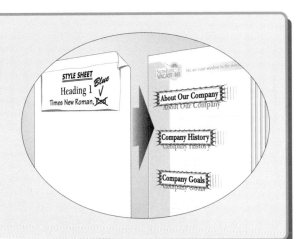

FOR MULTIPLE WEB PAGES

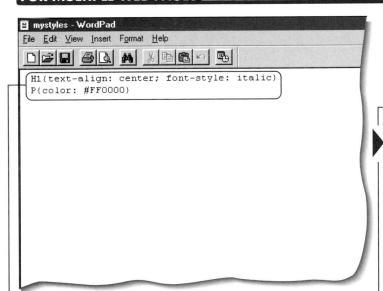

```
H1{text-align: center; font-style: italic}
P{color: #FF0000}
```

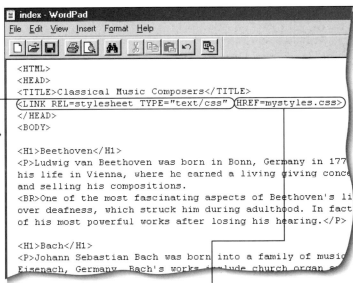

```
<HTML>
<HEAD>
<TITLE>Classical Music Composers</TITLE>
<LINK REL=stylesheet TYPE="text/css" HREF=mystyles.css>
</HEAD>
<BODY>

<H1>Beethoven</H1>
<P>Ludwig van Beethoven was born in Bonn, Germany in 177
his life in Vienna, where he earned a living giving conce
and selling his compositions.
<BR>One of the most fascinating aspects of Beethoven's li
over deafness, which struck him during adulthood. In fact
of his most powerful works after losing his hearing.</P>

<H1>Bach</H1>
<P>Johann Sebastian Bach was born into a family of music
Eisenach, Germany. Bach's works include church organ s
```

1 Create a new document in a word processor or text editor.

2 Perform steps **2** to **5** on page 174 to set up the information for the style sheet.

3 Save the document in the text-only format. Use the .css extension to name the document (example: mystyles.css).

Note: To save a document in the text-only format using Microsoft WordPad, perform steps 4 to 8 on page 28.

You must perform the following steps on each Web page you want to use the style sheet.

4 Type **<LINK REL=stylesheet TYPE="text/css"** between the <HEAD> and </HEAD> tags. Then press the **Spacebar**.

5 Type **HREF=?>** replacing **?** with the location of the style sheet on your computer.

Note: You can specify the location of a style sheet as you would specify the location of an image. For more information, see page 71.

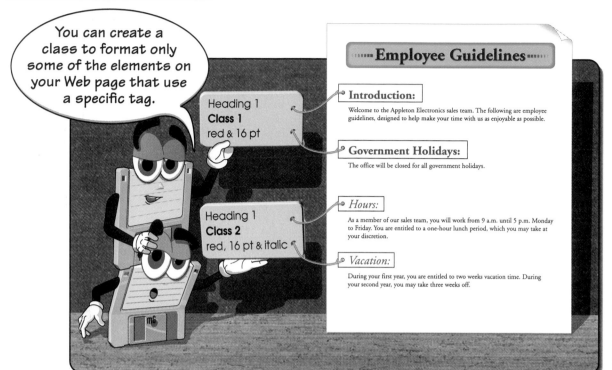

You can create a class to format only some of the elements on your Web page that use a specific tag.

Heading 1
Class 1
red & 16 pt

Heading 1
Class 2
red, 16 pt & italic

······ **Employee Guidelines** ······

Introduction:

Welcome to the Appleton Electronics sales team. The following are employee guidelines, designed to help make your time with us as enjoyable as possible.

Government Holidays:

The office will be closed for all government holidays.

Hours:

As a member of our sales team, you will work from 9 a.m. until 5 p.m. Monday to Friday. You are entitled to a one-hour lunch period, which you may take at your discretion.

Vacation:

During your first year, you are entitled to two weeks vacation time. During your second year, you may take three weeks off.

For example, you can create a class for elements that use tags such as H1 (H1 headings), P (paragraphs) or B (bold text).

CREATE A CLASS

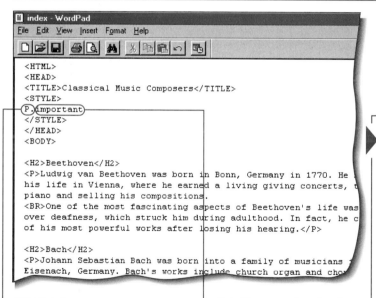

```
index - WordPad
File  Edit  View  Insert  Format  Help

<HTML>
<HEAD>
<TITLE>Classical Music Composers</TITLE>
<STYLE>
P.important
</STYLE>
</HEAD>
<BODY>

<H2>Beethoven</H2>
<P>Ludwig van Beethoven was born in Bonn, Germany in 1770. He
his life in Vienna, where he earned a living giving concerts, t
piano and selling his compositions.
<BR>One of the most fascinating aspects of Beethoven's life was
over deafness, which struck him during adulthood. In fact, he c
of his most powerful works after losing his hearing.</P>

<H2>Bach</H2>
<P>Johann Sebastian Bach was born into a family of musicians
Eisenach, Germany. Bach's works include church organ and cho
```

SET UP A CLASS

1 Between the <STYLE> and </STYLE> tags, type the tag you want to create a class for, followed by a period (.).

Note: You can create a class for tags such as H1 (H1 headings), P (paragraphs) and B (bold text).

2 Type a name for the class you want to create.

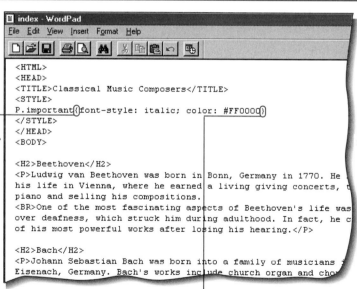

```
index - WordPad
File  Edit  View  Insert  Format  Help

<HTML>
<HEAD>
<TITLE>Classical Music Composers</TITLE>
<STYLE>
P.important{font-style: italic; color: #FF0000}
</STYLE>
</HEAD>
<BODY>

<H2>Beethoven</H2>
<P>Ludwig van Beethoven was born in Bonn, Germany in 1770. He
his life in Vienna, where he earned a living giving concerts, t
piano and selling his compositions.
<BR>One of the most fascinating aspects of Beethoven's life was
over deafness, which struck him during adulthood. In fact, he c
of his most powerful works after losing his hearing.</P>

<H2>Bach</H2>
<P>Johann Sebastian Bach was born into a family of musicians
Eisenach, Germany. Bach's works include church organ and cho
```

3 Type { to begin the characteristics for the class.

4 Type } to end the characteristics for the class.

Note: You can enter characteristics for the class between the brackets { }. A semi-colon (;) must separate each characteristic. To add characteristics, see pages 179 to 189.

Why would I create a class?

Creating a class gives you more control over the formatting and layout of information on your Web page. For example, you can create a class of important paragraphs (P.important) that will display slightly different formatting than regular paragraphs (P). The P.important paragraphs will display the formatting you define for regular (P) paragraphs as well as the formatting you define for P.important paragraphs.

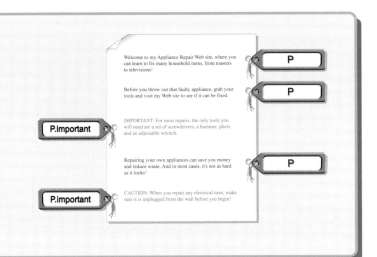

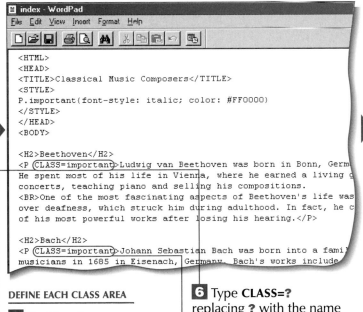

```
index - WordPad
File  Edit  View  Insert  Format  Help

<HTML>
<HEAD>
<TITLE>Classical Music Composers</TITLE>
<STYLE>
P.important{font-style: italic; color: #FF0000}
</STYLE>
</HEAD>
<BODY>

<H2>Beethoven</H2>
<P CLASS=important>Ludwig van Beethoven was born in Bonn, Germ
He spent most of his life in Vienna, where he earned a living
concerts, teaching piano and selling his compositions.
<BR>One of the most fascinating aspects of Beethoven's life was
over deafness, which struck him during adulthood. In fact, he c
of his most powerful works after losing his hearing.</P>

<H2>Bach</H2>
<P CLASS=important>Johann Sebastian Bach was born into a famil
musicians in 1685 in Eisenach, Germany. Bach's works include
```

DEFINE EACH CLASS AREA

5 Position the cursor in the tag before an element you want to include in the class.

Note: The element must use the tag you typed in step 1.

6 Type **CLASS=?** replacing **?** with the name of the class you typed in step **2**.

7 Repeat steps **5** and **6** for each element you want to include in the class.

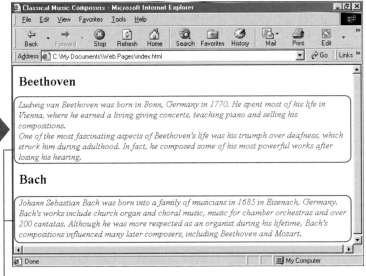

Beethoven

Ludwig van Beethoven was born in Bonn, Germany in 1770. He spent most of his life in Vienna, where he earned a living giving concerts, teaching piano and selling his compositions.
One of the most fascinating aspects of Beethoven's life was his triumph over deafness, which struck him during adulthood. In fact, he composed some of his most powerful works after losing his hearing.

Bach

Johann Sebastian Bach was born into a family of musicians in 1685 in Eisenach, Germany. Bach's works include church organ and choral music, music for chamber orchestras and over 200 cantatas. Although he was more respected as an organist during his lifetime, Bach's compositions influenced many later composers, including Beethoven and Mozart.

■ The Web browser displays each element you included in the class with the formatting you specified.

■ To display your Web page in a Web browser, see pages 32 to 35.

You can hide a style sheet from older Web browsers that cannot understand style sheets.

If you do not hide a style sheet from older Web browsers, the information for the style sheet may appear on your Web page.

HIDE A STYLE SHEET

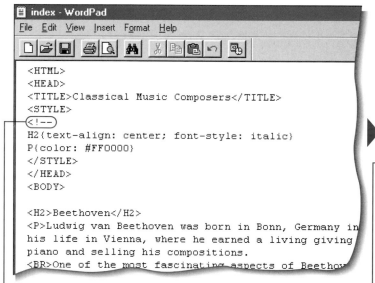

```
<HTML>
<HEAD>
<TITLE>Classical Music Composers</TITLE>
<STYLE>
<!--
H2{text-align: center; font-style: italic}
P{color: #FF0000}
</STYLE>
</HEAD>
<BODY>

<H2>Beethoven</H2>
<P>Ludwig van Beethoven was born in Bonn, Germany in
his life in Vienna, where he earned a living giving
piano and selling his compositions.
<BR>One of the most fascinating aspects of Beethov
```

1 Type **<!--** directly below the <STYLE> tag.

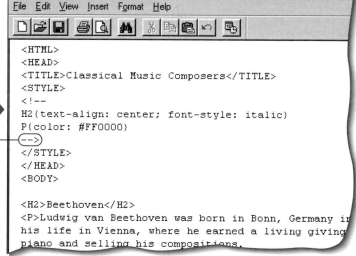

```
<HTML>
<HEAD>
<TITLE>Classical Music Composers</TITLE>
<STYLE>
<!--
H2{text-align: center; font-style: italic}
P{color: #FF0000}
-->
</STYLE>
</HEAD>
<BODY>

<H2>Beethoven</H2>
<P>Ludwig van Beethoven was born in Bonn, Germany in
his life in Vienna, where he earned a living giving
piano and selling his compositions.
```

2 Type **-->** directly above the </STYLE> tag.

■ If a reader displays your Web page in an older Web browser that cannot understand style sheets, the Web browser will ignore the style sheet information.

You can change the alignment of all the text on your Web page that uses a specific tag.

CHANGE TEXT ALIGNMENT

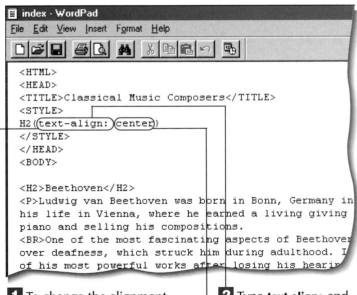

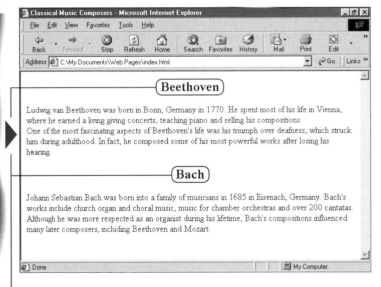

1 To change the alignment of all the text that uses a specific tag, position the cursor between the brackets { } for the tag.

Note: To set up a style sheet, see page 174.

2 Type **text-align:** and then press the **Spacebar**.

3 Type the way you want to align the text (**left**, **center**, **right** or **justify**).

■ The Web browser displays all the text that uses the tag with the alignment you specified.

■ To display your Web page in a Web browser, see pages 32 to 35.

Fruit & Flowers, Inc.

Freshly Picked Fruit   **Fresh Cut Flowers**

Our fruit selection includes popular berries such as strawberries and raspberries. We also carry exotic fruit such as mangos, papayas and kiwis.

Our flower selection includes seasonal plants such as poinsettias and mistletoe. We also carry tropical flowers such as orchids and yellow jasmine.

<P> BOLD

<P> BOLD

You can bold or italicize all the text on your Web page that uses a specific tag.

Bolding or italicizing text is useful for emphasizing information on your Web page.

BOLD TEXT

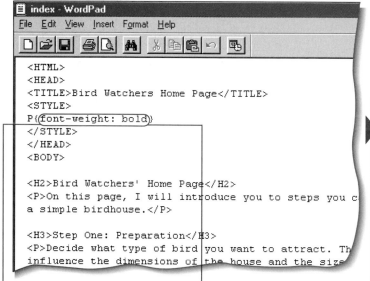

```
<HTML>
<HEAD>
<TITLE>Bird Watchers Home Page</TITLE>
<STYLE>
P{font-weight: bold}
</STYLE>
</HEAD>
<BODY>

<H2>Bird Watchers' Home Page</H2>
<P>On this page, I will introduce you to steps you c
a simple birdhouse.</P>

<H3>Step One: Preparation</H3>
<P>Decide what type of bird you want to attract. Th
influence the dimensions of the house and the size
```

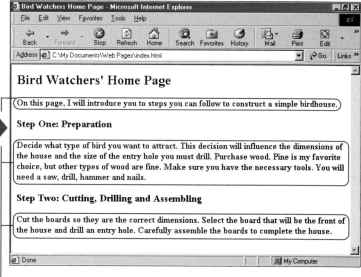

Bird Watchers' Home Page

On this page, I will introduce you to steps you can follow to construct a simple birdhouse.

Step One: Preparation

Decide what type of bird you want to attract. This decision will influence the dimensions of the house and the size of the entry hole you must drill. Purchase wood. Pine is my favorite choice, but other types of wood are fine. Make sure you have the necessary tools. You will need a saw, drill, hammer and nails.

Step Two: Cutting, Drilling and Assembling

Cut the boards so they are the correct dimensions. Select the board that will be the front of the house and drill an entry hole. Carefully assemble the boards to complete the house.

1 To bold all the text that uses a specific tag, position the cursor between the brackets { } for the tag.

Note: To set up a style sheet, see page 174.

2 Type **font-weight: bold**.

■ The Web browser bolds all the text that uses the tag.

■ To display your Web page in a Web browser, see pages 32 to 35.

Can I remove bold formatting from my Web page?

You can remove bold formatting from all the text on your Web page that uses a specific tag. For example, you can remove bold formatting from text using a tag that automatically bolds text, such as B (bold) or H1 (H1 headings).

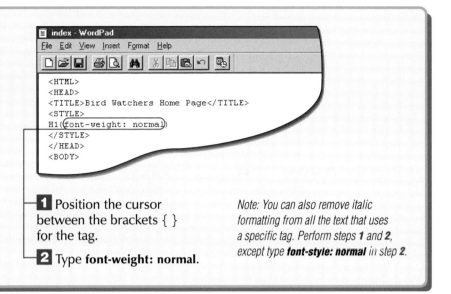

```
<HTML>
<HEAD>
<TITLE>Bird Watchers Home Page</TITLE>
<STYLE>
H1{font-weight: normal}
</STYLE>
</HEAD>
<BODY>
```

1 Position the cursor between the brackets { } for the tag.

2 Type **font-weight: normal**.

*Note: You can also remove italic formatting from all the text that uses a specific tag. Perform steps **1** and **2**, except type **font-style: normal** in step **2**.*

ITALICIZE TEXT

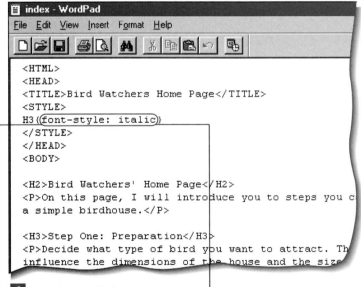

```
<HTML>
<HEAD>
<TITLE>Bird Watchers Home Page</TITLE>
<STYLE>
H3{font-style: italic}
</STYLE>
</HEAD>
<BODY>

<H2>Bird Watchers' Home Page</H2>
<P>On this page, I will introduce you to steps you c
a simple birdhouse.</P>

<H3>Step One: Preparation</H3>
<P>Decide what type of bird you want to attract. Th
influence the dimensions of the house and the size
```

1 To italicize all the text that uses a specific tag, position the cursor between the brackets { } for the tag.

Note: To set up a style sheet, see page 174.

2 Type **font-style: italic**.

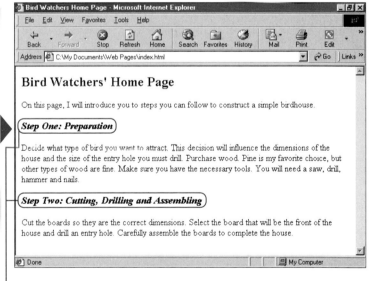

Bird Watchers' Home Page

On this page, I will introduce you to steps you can follow to construct a simple birdhouse.

Step One: Preparation

Decide what type of bird you want to attract. This decision will influence the dimensions of the house and the size of the entry hole you must drill. Purchase wood. Pine is my favorite choice, but other types of wood are fine. Make sure you have the necessary tools. You will need a saw, drill, hammer and nails.

Step Two: Cutting, Drilling and Assembling

Cut the boards so they are the correct dimensions. Select the board that will be the front of the house and drill an entry hole. Carefully assemble the boards to complete the house.

■ The Web browser italicizes all the text that uses the tag.

■ To display your Web page in a Web browser, see pages 32 to 35.

You can change the font of all the text on your Web page that uses a specific tag.

CHANGE THE FONT

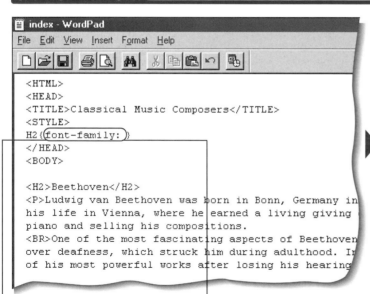

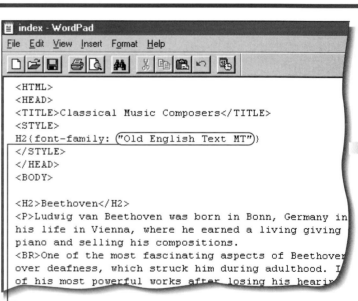

1 To change the font of all the text that uses a specific tag, position the cursor between the brackets { } for the tag.

Note: To set up a style sheet, see page 174.

2 Type **font-family:** and then press the **Spacebar**.

3 Type the name of the font you want to use, enclosed in quotation marks (" ").

■ Instead of typing the name of a font, you can specify a font type (**serif**, **sans-serif** or **monospace**).

182

Why should I specify more than one font?

You should specify more than one font in case your first font choice is not available on a reader's computer. One of the fonts you specify should be a common font, such as Arial, to increase the probability that your Web page will display one of your font choices.

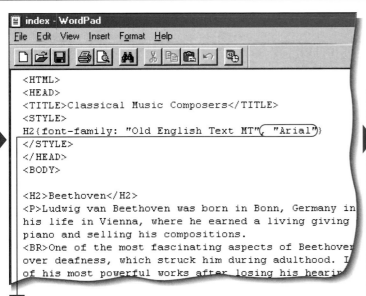

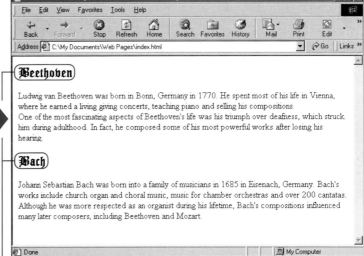

4 To specify a second font choice, type a comma (,) and then press the **Spacebar**. Then type your second font choice, enclosed in quotation marks (" ").

Note: For information on specifying more than one font, see the top of this page.

■ The Web browser displays all the text that uses the tag in the font you specified.

■ To display your Web page in a Web browser, see pages 32 to 35.

You can change the font size of all the text on your Web page that uses a specific tag.

Larger text is easier to read, but smaller text allows you to fit more information on a screen.

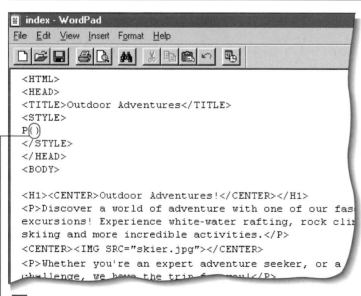

```
index - WordPad
File  Edit  View  Insert  Format  Help

<HTML>
<HEAD>
<TITLE>Outdoor Adventures</TITLE>
<STYLE>
P{ }
</STYLE>
</HEAD>
<BODY>

<H1><CENTER>Outdoor Adventures!</CENTER></H1>
<P>Discover a world of adventure with one of our fas
excursions! Experience white-water rafting, rock cli
skiing and more incredible activities.</P>
<CENTER><IMG SRC="skier.jpg"></CENTER>
<P>Whether you're an expert adventure seeker, or a
challenge, we have the trip f       you!</P>
```

1 To change the font size of all the text that uses a specific tag, position the cursor between the brackets { } for the tag.

Note: To set up a style sheet, see page 174.

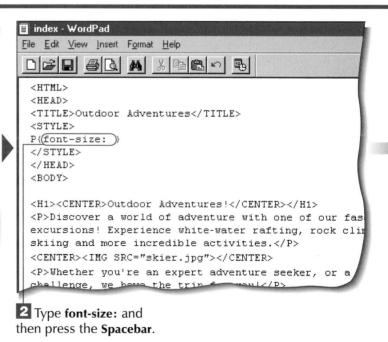

```
index - WordPad
File  Edit  View  Insert  Format  Help

<HTML>
<HEAD>
<TITLE>Outdoor Adventures</TITLE>
<STYLE>
P{font-size: }
</STYLE>
</HEAD>
<BODY>

<H1><CENTER>Outdoor Adventures!</CENTER></H1>
<P>Discover a world of adventure with one of our fas
excursions! Experience white-water rafting, rock cli
skiing and more incredible activities.</P>
<CENTER><IMG SRC="skier.jpg"></CENTER>
<P>Whether you're an expert adventure seeker, or a
challenge, we have the trip f       you!</P>
```

2 Type **font-size:** and then press the **Spacebar**.

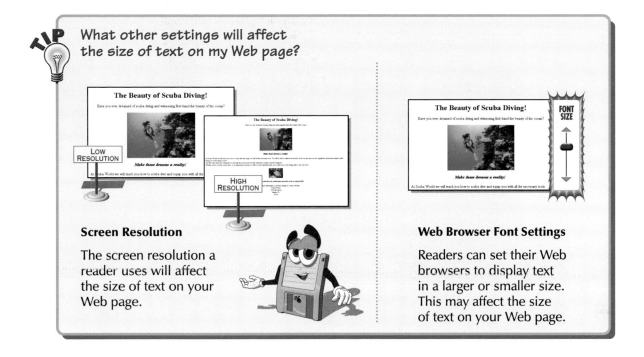

What other settings will affect the size of text on my Web page?

Screen Resolution

The screen resolution a reader uses will affect the size of text on your Web page.

Web Browser Font Settings

Readers can set their Web browsers to display text in a larger or smaller size. This may affect the size of text on your Web page.

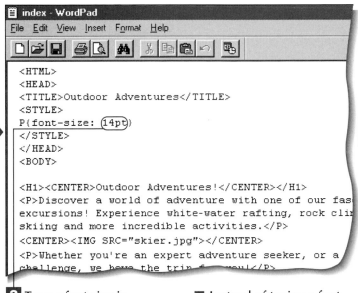

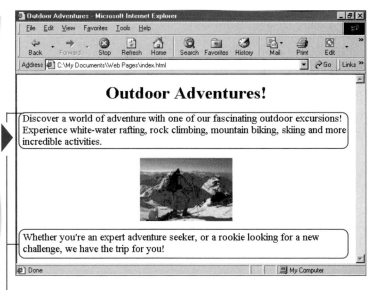

3 Type a font size in points or pixels (example: 14pt or 18px).

■ Instead of typing a font size in points or pixels, you can specify a descriptive font size (**xx-small**, **x-small**, **small**, **medium**, **large**, **x-large** or **xx-large**).

■ The Web browser displays all the text that uses the tag in the size you specified.

■ To display your Web page in a Web browser, see pages 32 to 35.

You can change the color of all the text on your Web page that uses a specific tag.

CHANGE TEXT COLOR

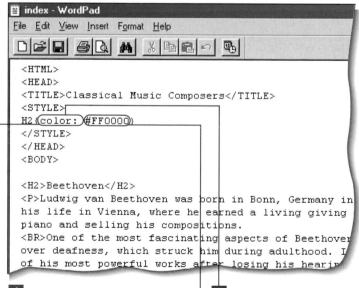

```
<HTML>
<HEAD>
<TITLE>Classical Music Composers</TITLE>
<STYLE>
H2 {color: #FF0000}
</STYLE>
</HEAD>
<BODY>

<H2>Beethoven</H2>
<P>Ludwig van Beethoven was born in Bonn, Germany in
his life in Vienna, where he earned a living giving
piano and selling his compositions.
<BR>One of the most fascinating aspects of Beethove
over deafness, which struck him during adulthood. I
of his most powerful works after losing his hearin
```

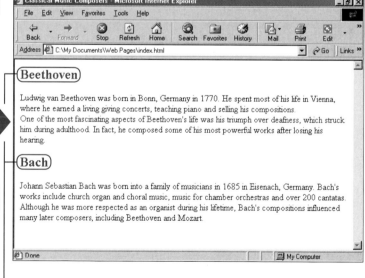

1 To change the color of all the text that uses a specific tag, position the cursor between the brackets { } for the tag.

Note: To set up a style sheet, see page 174.

2 Type **color:** and then press the **Spacebar**.

3 Type the name or code for the color you want to use (example: red or #FF0000).

Note: For a list of colors, see the top of page 57.

■ The Web browser displays all the text that uses the tag in the color you specified.

■ To display your Web page in a Web browser, see pages 32 to 35.

SET THE WIDTH AND HEIGHT

You can set the width and height of every element on your Web page that uses a specific tag.

For example, you can set the width and height of all your images (IMG) or the width of all your paragraphs (P). Netscape Navigator cannot currently use the width and height settings you specify for images.

SET THE WIDTH AND HEIGHT

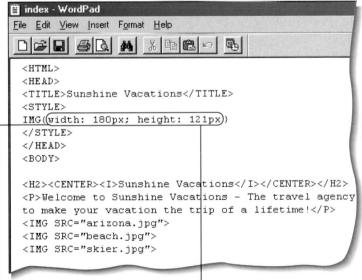

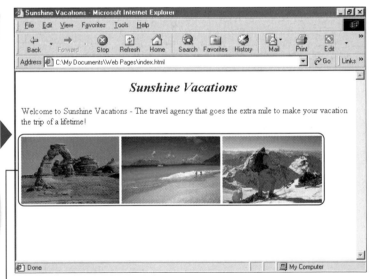

1 To set the width and height of every element that uses a specific tag, position the cursor between the brackets { } for the tag.

Note: To set up a style sheet, see page 174.

2 Type **width: ?; height: ?** replacing **?** with a width and height in pixels (example: 300px) or as a percentage of the window (example: 50%).

■ The Web browser displays every element that uses the tag with the width and height you specified.

■ To display your Web page in a Web browser, see pages 32 to 35.

*Note: You can set the width or height individually by specifying only a width or height in step **2**. Make sure you leave out the semi-colon (;).*

You can add a background color or image to every element on your Web page that uses a specific tag.

For example, you can add a background to elements such as headings (H1 to H6) and paragraphs (P).

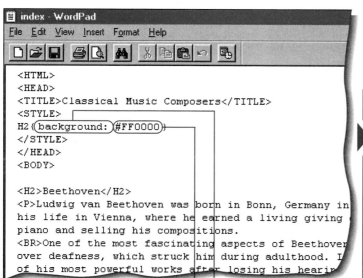

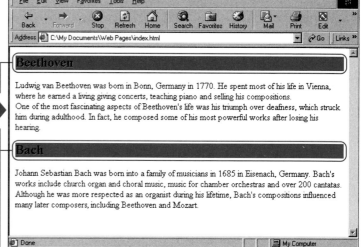

ADD A BACKGROUND COLOR

1 To add a background to every element that uses a specific tag, position the cursor between the brackets { } for the tag.

Note: To set up a style sheet, see page 174.

2 Type **background:** and then press the **Spacebar**.

3 Type the name or code for the color you want to use (example: red or #FF0000).

Note: For a list of colors, see the top of page 57.

■ The Web browser displays every element that uses the tag with the background color you specified.

■ To display your Web page in a Web browser, see pages 32 to 35.

188

Where can I obtain a background image?

You can obtain interesting background images at the following Web sites:

imagine.metanet.com

www.ip.pt/webground/main.htm

www.nepthys.com/textures

Make sure the background image you select does not make the text on your Web page difficult to read.

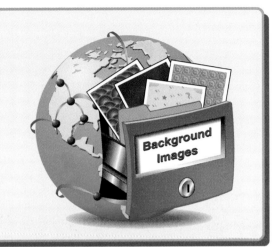

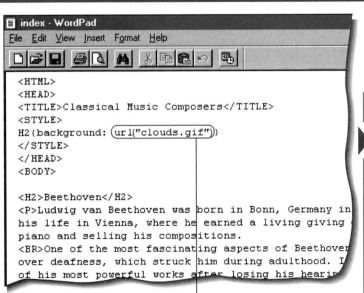

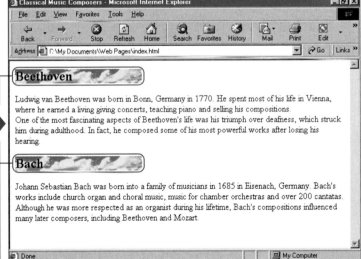

ADD A BACKGROUND IMAGE

1 Perform steps **1** and **2** on page 188.

2 Type **url("?")** replacing **?** with the location of the background image on your computer.

Note: For information on specifying the location of an image, see page 71.

■ The Web browser displays every element that uses the tag with the background image you specified.

■ To display your Web page in a Web browser, see pages 32 to 35.

■ The background image repeats until it fills the background area of every element.

CHAPTER 12

PUBLISH WEB PAGES

Are you ready to publish your Web pages? This chapter will show you how.

Web presence providers are companies that store Web pages and make them available on the Web.

Web presence providers store Web pages on computers called Web servers. Web servers store, monitor and control access to Web pages.

INTERNET SERVICE PROVIDERS

Internet service providers are companies that offer people access to the Internet. Most Internet service providers offer space on their Web servers where customers can publish their Web pages free of charge.

COMMERCIAL ONLINE SERVICES

Commercial online services such as America Online and The Microsoft Network will publish Web pages created by customers for free. Many commercial online services offer easy-to-use programs to help people create and publish Web pages.

FREE WEB PRESENCE PROVIDERS

There are many companies on the Web that will publish your Web pages for free. These companies offer a limited amount of storage space and may place advertisements on your Web pages.

You can find companies that will publish your Web pages for free at the following Web sites:

xoom.com

www.geocities.com

www.tripod.com

DEDICATED WEB PRESENCE PROVIDERS

Dedicated Web presence providers are companies that specialize in publishing Web pages for a fee. Dedicated Web presence providers are flexible and offer features that other Web presence providers do not offer.

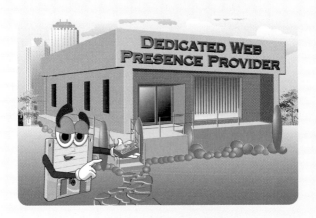

You can find dedicated Web presence providers at the following Web sites:

www.dreamhost.com

www.hostess.com

www.pair.com

YOUR OWN WEB SERVER

Purchasing your own Web server is the most expensive way to publish Web pages and requires a full-time connection to the Internet. Setting up and maintaining your own Web server is difficult, but will give you the greatest amount of control over your Web pages.

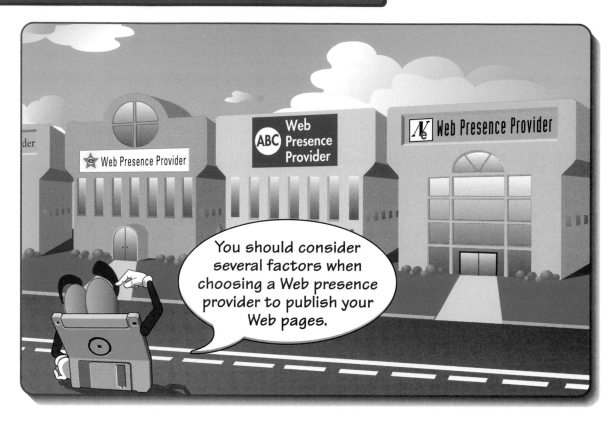

TECHNICAL SUPPORT

A Web presence provider should have a technical support department to answer your questions. You should be able to contact the department by telephone or by e-mail. A good technical support department will respond to questions you send by e-mail within a day.

TRAFFIC LIMIT

When readers view your Web pages, information transfers from the Web server to their computers. The amount of information that transfers depends on the number of people that view your Web pages and the file size of your pages.

Most Web presence providers limit the amount of information that can transfer in one day. If more information transfers, you may have to pay extra. You should choose a Web presence provider that allows at least 50 MB (megabytes) of information to transfer in one day.

RELIABILITY

Make sure the Web presence provider you choose is reliable. A Web presence provider should be able to tell you how often their Web servers shut down. You may want to ask a Web presence provider for customer references that you can contact. You should take into consideration that all Web presence providers occasionally shut down their Web servers for maintenance and upgrades.

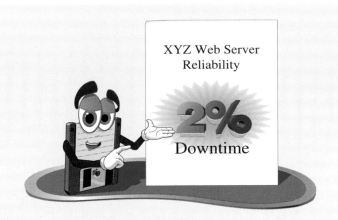

STORAGE SPACE

Most Web presence providers limit the amount of space you can use to store your Web pages. Choose a Web presence provider that allows you to store at least 5 MB (megabytes) of information.

ACCESS LOGS

A good Web presence provider will supply you with statistics about your Web pages, such as which Web pages are the most popular and where your readers are from. You can also view any error messages that readers may see when viewing your Web pages, such as "Page Not Found". Access logs can help you determine if you need to make changes to your Web pages.

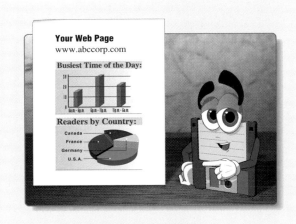

SHOPPING SOFTWARE

If you plan to use your Web pages to sell products on the Web, you should consider a Web presence provider that offers shopping software. Shopping software simplifies the task of creating Web pages that allow readers to purchase products. You can easily create Web pages that accept orders, verify credit card numbers, generate invoices and organize product shipments.

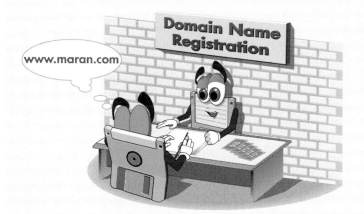

DOMAIN NAME REGISTRATION

For a fee, you can choose the address, or domain name, that people type to access your Web pages. A personalized domain name is easy for people to remember and will not change if you switch to another Web presence provider. Most Web presence providers will register a domain name for you for a fee.

DATABASE ACCESS

If you want to give readers access to a large amount of information, you should choose a Web presence provider that lets you use a database program on the Web server. A database program can store a large amount of information, such as a product list. When a reader requests information, the Web server will search the database for the information and then display the requested information on a Web page.

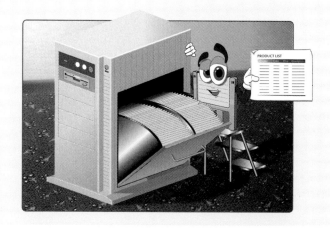

SECURE WEB SERVERS

Many Web presence providers offer secure Web servers. Secure Web servers allow you to publish Web pages that request confidential information from your readers, such as credit card information. Secure Web servers use special software to encode confidential information that transfers between readers and the Web server.

CGI SCRIPT ACCESS

Web pages can include forms that allow readers to send you questions and comments, order products or fill out questionnaires. If you plan to use forms on your Web pages, make sure your Web presence provider allows you to use CGI scripts. CGI scripts are programs that process information sent by a form.

SHELL ACCESS

Shell access allows you to edit your Web pages directly on a Web server. This lets you make changes to your Web pages without having to edit the pages on your computer and then transfer the updated pages to the Web server. Shell access allows you to edit your Web pages from any computer connected to the Internet, which is useful if you plan to update your Web pages from more than one location.

You can specify keywords to help search tools catalog your Web page.

KEYWORDS

Fishing
Fish
Tackle
Reel
Rod
Bait
Supplies
Line
Boat
Tackle Box
Hook
Spinner
Jig
Fly Fishing

When readers enter words in a search tool that match your keywords, your Web page will more likely appear in the search results.

SPECIFY KEYWORDS

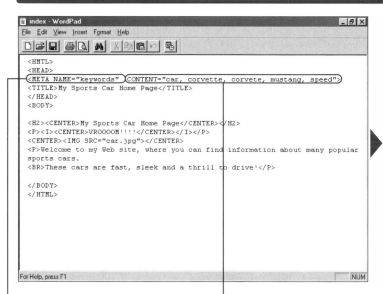

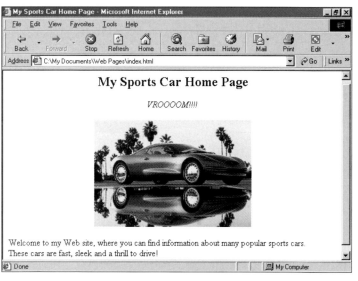

1 Directly below the <HEAD> tag, type **<META NAME="keywords"** and then press the **Spacebar**.

2 Type **CONTENT="?">** replacing **?** with a list of words that describe your Web page. Separate each word with a comma and a space.

■ Readers will not see the information in the META tag when they view your Web page.

■ To display your Web page in a Web browser, see pages 32 to 35.

■ You should use general and specific words to describe your Web page, such as "car" and "corvette." You may also want to include misspelled words that people may type, such as "corvete".

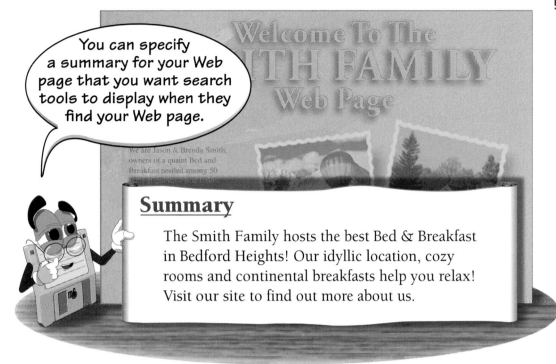

You can specify a summary for your Web page that you want search tools to display when they find your Web page.

Summary

The Smith Family hosts the best Bed & Breakfast in Bedford Heights! Our idyllic location, cozy rooms and continental breakfasts help you relax! Visit our site to find out more about us.

If you do not specify a summary, search tools will use the first few sentences on your Web page for the summary.

SPECIFY WEB PAGE SUMMARY

1 Directly below the <HEAD> tag, type **<META NAME="description"** and then press the **Spacebar**.

2 Type **CONTENT="?">** replacing **?** with a summary of your Web page.

Note: Try to limit the summary to one or two sentences.

■ Readers will not see the information in the META tag when they view your Web page.

■ To display your Web page in a Web browser, see pages 32 to 35.

CHECK WEB PAGE FILE NAMES

Your Web page file names should all have the .htm or .html extension (example: garden.html) and should not include spaces or unusual characters, such as * or &. You should check with your Web presence provider to ensure that you use the correct name for your home page. Home pages are usually named index.html.

ORGANIZE WEB PAGE FILES

You should store all of your Web pages in one folder on your computer. Make sure the folder also contains all the images, sounds, videos and other files you included on your Web pages. If the folder contains many files, you may want to store some of the files in subfolders. For example, you can store all the images for your Web pages in a subfolder.

CHECK FILE REFERENCES

After you organize your Web page files, you should check all references to the files on your Web pages.

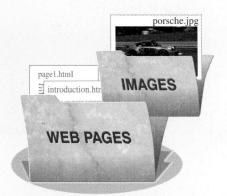

For example, if an image on a Web page is stored in the same folder as the Web page, make sure you specified just the name of the image (example: porsche.jpg).

If an image on a Web page is stored in a subfolder, make sure you specified both the name of the subfolder and the name of the image (example: images/porsche.jpg).

CHECK TOTAL FILE SIZE OF WEB PAGES

Make sure the total file size of all your Web pages does not exceed the amount of space that your Web presence provider allows. If the total file size is too large, an error message will appear when you try to transfer the Web pages.

OBTAIN AN FTP PROGRAM

You need a File Transfer Protocol (FTP) program to transfer your Web pages to a Web server. You can obtain popular FTP programs at the following Web sites:

WS_FTP Pro (Windows)
www.ipswitch.com

Fetch (Macintosh)
www.dartmouth.edu/pages/softdev/fetch.html

TRANSFER WEB PAGES TO WEB SERVER

You must transfer your Web pages to a Web server to make the pages available on the Web.

TRANSFER WEB PAGES TO WEB SERVER

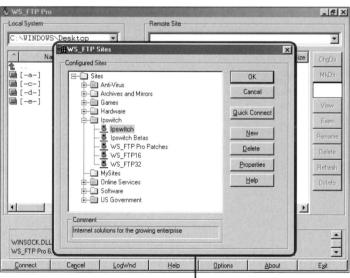

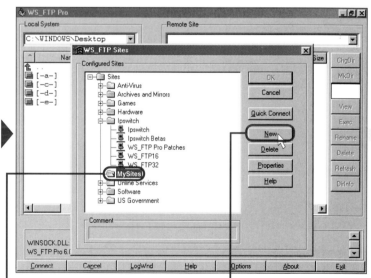

SET UP A CONNECTION

1 Start the FTP program you will use to transfer your Web pages to a Web server. In this example, we started WS_FTP Pro.

Note: For information on FTP programs, see page 201.

■ The WS_FTP Sites dialog box appears.

2 Click the **MySites** folder to add a new connection to this folder.

3 Click **New** to set up a new connection to your Web server.

■ The New Site/Folder dialog box appears.

What information do I need to transfer my Web pages to a Web server?

Before you can transfer your Web pages to a Web server, you must know the following information. If you do not know the information, ask your Web presence provider.

Web server address

User ID

Password

The name of the folder on the Web server where you will store your Web pages. In many cases, the folder is named **public**.

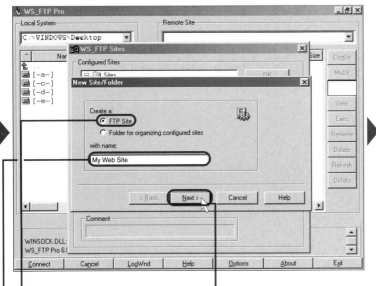

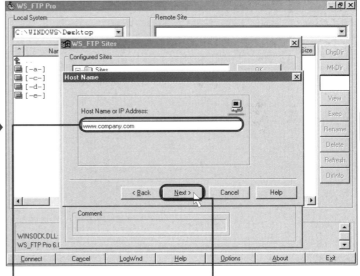

4 Click this option to set up a new connection (○ changes to ⊙).

5 Click this area and then type a name for the connection.

6 Click **Next** to continue.

7 Type the address of the Web server you want to transfer your Web pages to.

8 Click **Next** to continue.

CONTINUED

You only need to set up a connection to a Web server once. After you set up a connection, you can easily connect to the Web server at any time.

TRANSFER WEB PAGES TO WEB SERVER (CONTINUED)

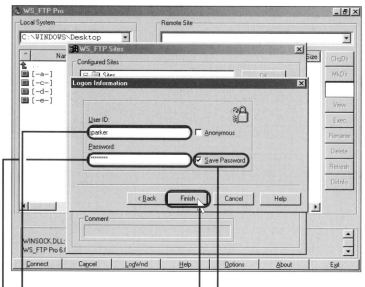

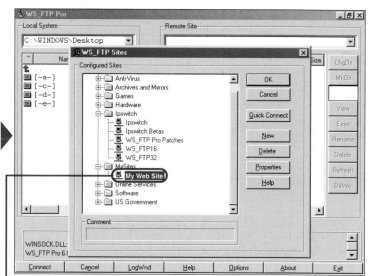

9 Type your user ID.

10 Click this area and then type your password. A symbol (×) appears for each character you type to prevent others from seeing your password.

11 To save your password so you will not need to retype the password again later, click this option (☐ changes to ☑).

12 Click **Finish**.

■ The program stores the information you entered for the connection and displays the name of the connection in this area.

Why was I disconnected from my Web server?

If you do not use the Web server for a period of time, the Web server will automatically disconnect you. This helps ensure that the Web server's resources will be available for other people who need to access the Web server.

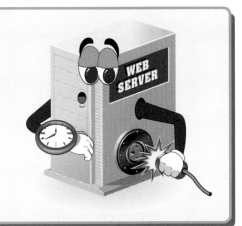

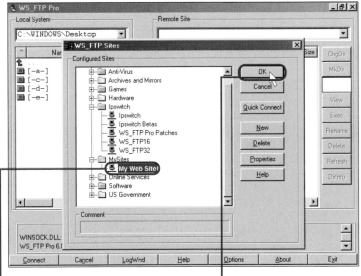

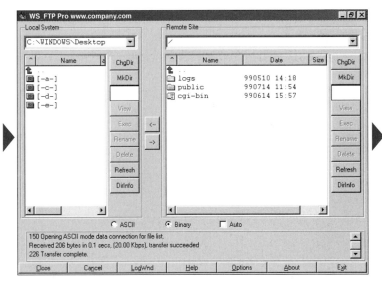

CONNECT TO WEB SERVER

1 Click the connection for the Web server you want to transfer your Web pages to.

2 Click **OK** to connect to the Web server.

■ You are now connected to the Web server.

CONTINUED

The time required to transfer your Web pages to a Web server depends on the connection speed, the file size of your Web pages and how busy the Web server is.

Most Web pages will transfer in a few seconds.

TRANSFER WEB PAGES TO WEB SERVER (CONTINUED)

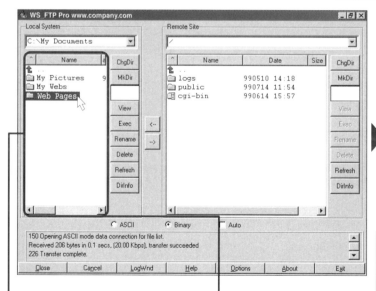

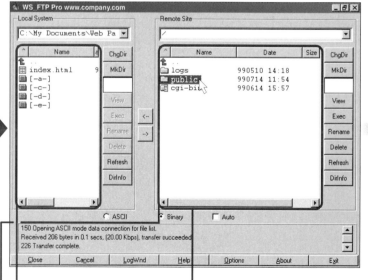

■ This area displays the folders and files stored on your computer.

3 Locate the folder that contains the Web page(s) you want to transfer to the Web server.

Note: You can double-click ⬆ to move up one level in the folder structure.

4 Double-click the folder to display the contents of the folder.

■ The contents of the folder appear.

■ This area displays the folders and files stored on the Web server.

5 Locate the folder you want to transfer your Web pages to. In many cases, the folder is named **public**.

6 Double-click the folder to display the contents of the folder.

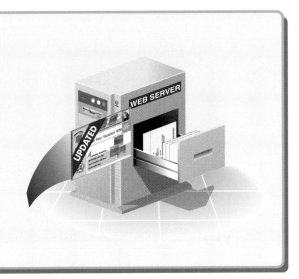

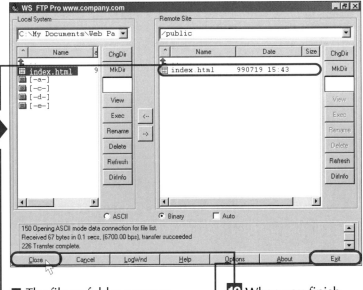

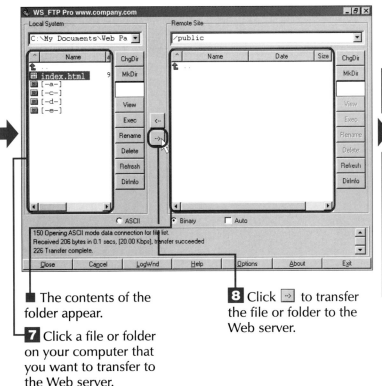

TIP

How do I update my Web pages on the Web server?

If you make changes to Web pages on your computer, you must transfer the updated pages to the Web server. The updated Web pages will replace the old Web pages on the Web server. To transfer the updated Web pages to the Web server, perform steps **1** to **11** starting on page 205. When you transfer the updated Web pages, an error message may appear indicating that the updated pages will replace the old pages.

■ The contents of the folder appear.

7 Click a file or folder on your computer that you want to transfer to the Web server.

8 Click → to transfer the file or folder to the Web server.

■ The file or folder appears on the Web server.

9 Repeat steps **7** and **8** for each file and folder you want to transfer.

10 When you finish transferring files and folders, click **Close** to end the connection to the Web server.

11 Click **Exit** to exit the program.

TEST YOUR WEB PAGES

> You should test your Web pages to make sure they look and work the way you planned.

Test your Web pages to see how easily you can browse through the information. Make sure your Web pages have a consistent design and writing style and do not contain formatting or layout errors.

CHECK LINKS

You should regularly check the links on your Web pages to make sure they will take your readers to the intended destinations. Make sure the linked Web pages still exist and contain useful information.

USE A VALIDATION SERVICE

You can use a validation service to check your Web pages for HTML errors. You can find a validation service at the validator.w3.org Web site.

TRANSFER SPEED

Determine how long your Web pages take to appear at different transfer speeds. Many people use modems that transfer information at 56 Kbps, but slower modems are still common. Web pages with large file sizes may take a long time to transfer.

TURN OFF IMAGES

Some people turn off the display of images to browse the Web more quickly, while others use Web browsers that cannot display images. You should view your Web pages without images to ensure that readers who do not see images will still find your pages useful.

VIEW AT DIFFERENT RESOLUTIONS

The resolution of a monitor determines the amount of information that will appear on a screen. Readers will view your Web pages at different resolutions. You should view your Web pages at the two most popular resolutions—640x480 and 800x600.

640 x 480   800 x 600

VIEW IN DIFFERENT WEB BROWSERS

You should view your Web pages in different Web browsers to make sure the pages look the way you planned. Each Web browser will display your Web pages in a slightly different way. Test your Web pages with the two most popular Web browsers—Microsoft Internet Explorer and Netscape Navigator.

Microsoft Internet Explorer   Netscape Navigator

VIEW ON DIFFERENT COMPUTERS

Web pages can look different when displayed on different computers. You should view your Web pages on different computers to ensure the pages appear the way you planned. You should also make sure any sounds, videos or other multimedia you added to the Web pages work the way you intended.

After you publish your Web pages, there are several ways you can let people know about the pages.

MAIL ANNOUNCEMENTS

You can mail an announcement about your Web pages to family, friends, colleagues and clients. You can also mail information about your Web pages to local newspapers and magazines that may be interested in your Web pages.

E-MAIL MESSAGES

Most e-mail programs include a feature, called a signature, that allows you to add the same information to the end of every e-mail message you send. You can use a signature to include information about your Web pages in all your e-mail messages.

EXCHANGE LINKS

If another page on the Web discusses ideas related to your Web pages, you can ask if they will include a link to your pages if you do the same. This allows people reading the other Web page to easily visit your Web pages.

WEB PAGE ADVERTISEMENTS

Many companies set aside areas on their Web pages where you can advertise your Web pages. The LinkExchange helps you advertise your Web pages free of charge. The LinkExchange is located at the adnetwork.linkexchange.com Web site.

NEWSGROUPS

You can send an announcement about your Web pages to discussion groups called newsgroups. Make sure you choose newsgroups that discuss topics related to your Web pages. You can announce new or updated Web pages to the comp.infosystems.www.announce newsgroup.

You can also announce your Web pages to discussion groups offered by Web sites.

MAILING LISTS

You can send an announcement to carefully selected mailing lists. A mailing list is a discussion group that communicates through e-mail. You should read the messages in a mailing list for a week before sending an announcement to make sure the mailing list members would be interested in your Web pages. You can find a directory of mailing lists at the www.liszt.com Web site.

SEARCH TOOLS

Search tools help people quickly find information on the Web. You can add your Web pages to various search tools so people can easily find your Web pages.

You can see a description of the top 100 search tools at the www.mmgco.com/top100.html Web site. You can add your Web pages to many search tools at once at the www.submit-it.com Web site.

CHAPTER 13

SUMMARY OF HTML TAGS

Would you like a summary of the HTML tags discussed throughout the book? This chapter organizes the HTML tags in a chart for easy reference.

Beethoven

Ludwig van Beethoven was born in Bonn, Germany in 1770. He spent most of his life in Vienna, where he earned a living giving concerts, teaching piano and writing his compositi

`<H2>` *Brush Script MT*

`<P>` Times New Roman

SUMMARY OF HTML TAGS

TAG/ATTRIBUTE	DESCRIPTION	PAGE REFERENCES

BASIC HTML TAGS

TAG/ATTRIBUTE	DESCRIPTION	PAGE REFERENCES
!--	Adds a comment	43
BODY	Identifies the main content of a Web page	31
BR	Starts a new line	38
H1 to H6	Creates headings	40
ALIGN	Aligns headings	41
HEAD	Contains information about a Web page	30
HTML	Identifies a document as an HTML document	30
META	Provides information about a Web page	198, 199
CONTENT	Specifies keywords or a summary for a Web page	198, 199
NAME	Adds information that helps search tools catalog and summarize a Web page	198, 199
P	Starts a new paragraph	36
ALIGN	Aligns a paragraph	37
TITLE	Creates a title for a Web page	31

FORMAT TEXT

TAG/ATTRIBUTE	DESCRIPTION	PAGE REFERENCES
B	Bolds text	48
BASEFONT	Changes the appearance of all text	54
SIZE	Changes the size of all text	54
BLOCKQUOTE	Separates a section of text from the main text	59
BODY		
BGCOLOR	Changes the background color of a Web page	58
TEXT	Changes the color of all text	56
CENTER	Centers text	39
FONT	Changes the appearance of text	52, 55, 57
COLOR	Changes the color of text	57
FACE	Changes the font of text	52
SIZE	Changes the size of text	55
I	Italicizes text	48
PRE	Retains the spacing of text you type	42
STRIKE	Places a line through text	49
SUB	Places text slightly below the main text	50
SUP	Places text slightly above the main text	50
TT	Creates typewriter text	51
U	Underlines text	49

FORMS

TAG/ATTRIBUTE	DESCRIPTION	PAGE REFERENCES
FORM	Creates a form	129
ACTION	Identifies the location of a CGI script for a form	129
METHOD	Specifies how information from a form transfers to a Web server	129
INPUT	Creates an item on a form	130, 134, 136, 138, 139
CHECKED	Selects a radio button or check box automatically	134, 137
MAXLENGTH	Specifies the maximum number of characters for a text box	131

TAG/ATTRIBUTE	DESCRIPTION	PAGE REFERENCES
FORMS (Continued)		
NAME	Identifies an item on a form to a Web server	130, 134, 136
SIZE	Specifies the size of a text box	131
TYPE	Specifies the type of an item on a form	130, 134, 136, 138, 139
VALUE	Identifies an item on a form	134, 136, 138, 139
TEXTAREA	Creates a large text area	132
COLS	Specifies a width for a large text area	133
NAME	Identifies a large text area to a Web server	132
ROWS	Specifies a height for a large text area	132
WRAP	Wraps text within a large text area	133
FRAMES		
A		
HREF	Specifies the location of a linked Web page to appear in a frame	168
TARGET	Specifies the frame where a linked Web page will appear	169
FRAME	Specifies the information for one frame	167
NAME	Names a frame	167
SRC	Specifies the location of a Web page that will appear in a frame	167
FRAMESET	Specifies the structure for frames	166
COLS	Creates frames in columns	166
ROWS	Creates frames in rows	166
IMAGE MAPS		
AREA	Specifies the information for one image area	162
COORDS	Specifies all the coordinates for one image area	162
HREF	Specifies the location of a Web page linked to an image area	163
SHAPE	Specifies the shape of one image area	162
IMG	Adds an image	70
USEMAP	Identifies the image map for an image	161
MAP	Creates an image map	161
NAME	Names an image map	161
IMAGES		
BODY		
BACKGROUND	Adds a background image to a Web page	80
BR		
CLEAR	Stops text from wrapping around an image	77
CENTER	Centers an image	72
HR	Adds a horizontal rule	82
ALIGN	Aligns a horizontal rule	85
SIZE	Changes the thickness of a horizontal rule	83
WIDTH	Changes the width of a horizontal rule	84

SUMMARY OF HTML TAGS

TAG/ATTRIBUTE	DESCRIPTION	PAGE REFERENCES
IMAGES (Continued)		
IMG	Adds an image	70
ALIGN	Aligns an image with text or wraps text around an image	75, 76
ALT	Displays alternative text when an image does not appear	74
BORDER	Adds a border to an image	73
HEIGHT	Specifies the height of an image	90
HSPACE	Adds space to the left and right sides of an image	78
SRC	Specifies the location of an image	70
VSPACE	Adds space above and below an image	79
WIDTH	Specifies the width of an image	90
JAVA APPLETS		
APPLET	Adds a Java applet	154
CODE	Specifies the location of a Java applet	154
HEIGHT	Specifies the height of a Java applet	154
WIDTH	Specifies the width of a Java applet	154
JAVASCRIPT		
NOSCRIPT	Displays alternative text when JavaScript does not run	159
SCRIPT	Adds JavaScript to a Web page	157
TYPE	Identifies a script as JavaScript	157
LINKS		
A	Creates a link	102, 103, 104, 106, 108
HREF	Specifies the location of a linked Web page or other item	102,103,106,108
NAME	Names a Web page area displayed by selecting a link	104
BODY		
LINK	Changes the color of an unvisited link	110
VLINK	Changes the color of a visited link	111
LISTS		
DD	Identifies a definition in a list	63
DL	Creates a list of terms with definitions	63
DT	Identifies a term in a list	63
LI	Identifies an item in an ordered or unordered list	60, 62
OL	Creates an ordered list	60
START	Specifies a starting number	61
TYPE	Specifies a number style	61
UL	Creates an unordered list	62

TAG/ATTRIBUTE	DESCRIPTION	PAGE REFERENCES
SOUNDS AND VIDEOS		
A		
HREF	Specifies the location of a linked sound or video	144, 148
EMBED	Adds a video to a Web page	150
AUTOSTART	Plays a video automatically	151
HEIGHT	Specifies the height of a video	150
LOOP	Plays a video continuously	151
SRC	Specifies the location of a video	150
WIDTH	Specifies the width of a video	150
STYLE SHEETS		
CLASS	Divides elements that use the same tag into groups	177
LINK	Links a Web page to a style sheet stored in a separate document	175
HREF	Specifies the location of a style sheet stored in a separate document	175
REL	Specifies a link to a style sheet	175
TYPE	Specifies the format of a style sheet	175
STYLE	Creates a style sheet	174
STYLE SHEET CHARACTERISTICS		
background	Specifies a background color or image for elements	188
color	Specifies a color for text	186
font-family	Specifies a font for text	182
font-size	Specifies a font size for text	184
font-style	Italicizes text	181
font-weight	Bolds text	180
height	Specifies a height for elements	187
text-align	Aligns text	179
width	Specifies a width for elements	187
TABLES		
CAPTION	Adds a caption to a table	121
CENTER	Centers a table	119
TABLE	Creates a table	116
BORDER	Adds a border to a table	120
TD	Creates a data cell	117
COLSPAN	Combines two or more data cells across a column	122
ROWSPAN	Combines two or more data cells down a row	123
TH	Creates a header cell	117
COLSPAN	Combines two or more header cells across a column	122
ROWSPAN	Combines two or more header cells down a row	123
TR	Creates a row in a table	116
ALIGN	Horizontally aligns data in a table	124
VALIGN	Vertically aligns data in a table	125

INDEX

INDEX

OVER 6 MILLION

 OTHER **3-D Visual** SERIES

SIMPLIFIED SERIES

ALSO AVAILABLE!

Microsoft® Office 2000 Simplified

ISBN 0-7645-6052-2
$29.99 USA/£28.99 UK
$39.99 CAN

Microsoft Word 2000 Simplified
ISBN 0-7645-6054-9
$24.99 USA/£23.99 UK
$32.99 CAN

Microsoft Excel 2000 Simplified
ISBN 0-7645-6053-0
$24.99 USA/£23.99 UK
$32.99 CAN

Microsoft Access 2000 Simplified
ISBN 0-7645-6058-1
$24.99 USA/£23.99 UK
$32.99 CAN

Internet and World Wide Web Simplified, 3rd Edition
ISBN 0-7645-3409-2
$24.99 USA/£23.99 UK
$32.99 CAN

Word For Windows 95 Simplified
ISBN 1-56884-681-9
$19.99 USA/£18.99 UK
$29.99 CAN

Word 6 For Windows Simplified
ISBN 1-56884-660-6
$19.99 USA/£18.99 UK
$29.99 CAN

Excel 97 Simplified
ISBN 0-7645-6022-0
$24.99 USA/£23.99 UK
$32.99 CAN

Excel For Windows 95 Simplified
ISBN 1-56884-682-7
$19.99 USA/£18.99 UK
$29.99 CAN

Excel 5 For Windows Simplified
ISBN 1-56884-664-9
$19.99 USA/£18.99 UK
$29.99 CAN

Office 97 Simplified
ISBN 0-7645-6009-3
$29.99 USA/£28.99 UK
$39.99 CAN

POCKETGUIDES

The Proven 3-D Visual Approach To Learning Computers In A Handy Pocket Size.

Windows 98 Visual PocketGuide
ISBN 0-7645-6035-2
$16.99 USA/£15.99 UK
$23.99 CAN

Windows 95 Visual PocketGuide
ISBN 1-56884-661-4
$14.99 USA/£13.99 UK
$21.99 CAN

ALSO AVAILABLE:

Windows 3.1 Visual PocketGuide
ISBN 1-56884-650-9
$14.99 USA/£13.99 UK
$21.99 CAN

 ...Visit our Web site at **www.maran.com**

S A T I S F I E D   U S E R S !

from:
maranGraphics™
& IDG BOOKS

Windows 98 Simplified

ISBN 0-7645-6030-1
$24.99 USA/£23.99 UK
$32.99 CAN

MORE Windows 98 Simplified

ISBN 0-7645-6037-9
$24.99 USA/£23.99 UK
$32.99 CAN

Windows 95 Simplified

ISBN 1-56884-662-2
$19.99 USA/£18.99 UK
$29.99 CAN

MORE Windows 95 Simplified

ISBN 1-56884-689-4
$19.99 USA/£18.99 UK
$29.99 CAN

Windows 3.1 Simplified

ISBN 1-56884-654-1
$19.99 USA/£18.99 UK
$29.99 CAN

Word 97 Simplified

ISBN 0-7645-6011-5
$24.99 USA/£23.99 UK
$32.99 CAN

WordPerfect 6.1 For Windows Simplified

ISBN 1-56884-665-7
$19.99 USA/£18.99 UK
$29.99 CAN

Creating Web Pages Simplified

ISBN 0-7645-6007-7
$24.99 USA/£23.99 UK
$32.99 CAN

Computers Simplified, 4th Edition

ISBN 0-7645-6042-5
$24.99 USA/£23.99 UK
$32.99 CAN

America Online Simplified

ISBN 0-7645-6033-6
$24.99 USA/£23.99 UK
$32.99 CAN

PC Upgrade and Repair Simplified

ISBN 0-7645-6049-2
$24.99 USA/£23.99 UK
$32.99 CAN

FOR CORPORATE ORDERS, PLEASE CALL: **1-800-469-6616**

OVER 6 MILLION

OTHER 3-D Visual SERIES

TEACH YOURSELF VISUALLY SERIES

ALSO AVAILABLE!
Teach Yourself Microsoft® Office 2000 VISUALLY

ISBN 0-7645-6051-4
$29.99 USA/£28.99 UK
$39.99 CAN

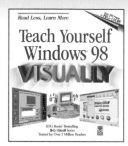

Teach Yourself Windows 98 VISUALLY

ISBN 0-7645-6025-5
$29.99 USA/£28.99 UK
$39.99 CAN

Teach Yourself MORE Windows 98 VISUALLY

ISBN 0-7645-6044-1
$29.99 USA/£28.99 UK
$39.99 CAN

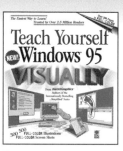

Teach Yourself Windows 95 VISUALLY

ISBN 0-7645-6001-8
$29.99 USA/£28.99 UK
$39.99 CAN

Teach Yourself Windows NT 4 VISUALLY

ISBN 0-7645-6061-1
$29.99 USA/£28.99 UK
$39.99 CAN

Teach Yourself Computers and the Internet VISUALLY, 2nd Edition

ISBN 0-7645-6041-7
$29.99 USA/£28.99 UK
$39.99 CAN

Teach Yourself Networking VISUALLY

ISBN 0-7645-6023-9
$29.99 USA/£28.99 UK
$39.99 CAN

Teach Yourself Office 97 VISUALLY

ISBN 0-7645-6018-2
$29.99 USA/£28.99 UK
$39.99 CAN

Teach Yourself Access 97 VISUALLY

ISBN 0-7645-6026-3
$29.99 USA/£28.99 UK
$39.99 CAN

Teach Yourself Netscape Navigator 4 VISUALLY

ISBN 0-7645-6028-X
$29.99 USA/£28.99 UK
$39.99 CAN

ALSO AVAILABLE!

Teach Yourself Microsoft Excel 2000 VISUALLY

ISBN 0-7645-6056-5
$29.99 USA/£28.99 UK
$39.99 CAN

Teach Yourself Microsoft Access 2000 VISUALLY

ISBN 0-7645-6059-X
$29.99 USA/£28.99 UK
$39.99 CAN

Teach Yourself Microsoft Word 2000 VISUALLY

ISBN 0-7645-6055-7
$29.99 USA/£28.99 UK
$39.99 CAN

Teach Yourself Microsoft PowerPoint 2000 VISUALLY

ISBN 0-7645-6060-3
$29.99 USA/£28.99 UK
$39.99 CAN

 ...Visit our Web site at www.maran.com

SATISFIED USERS!

from:

maranGraphics™
& IDG BOOKS

MASTER VISUALLY SERIES

Teach Yourself Microsoft PowerPoint 97 VISUALLY

ISBN 0-7645-6062-X
$29.99 USA/£28.99 UK
$39.99 CAN

Teach Yourself Microsoft Excel 97 VISUALLY

ISBN 0-7645-6063-8
$29.99 USA/£28.99 UK
$39.99 CAN

Master Windows 98 VISUALLY

ISBN 0-7645-6034-4
$39.99 USA/£36.99 UK
$54.99 CAN

Master Windows 95 VISUALLY

ISBN 0-7645-6024-7
$39.99 USA/£36.99 UK
$54.99 CAN

Teach Yourself Word 97 VISUALLY

ISBN 0-7645-6032-8
$29.99 USA/£28.99 UK
$39.99 CAN

Teach Yourself the Internet and World Wide Web VISUALLY

ISBN 0-7645-6020-4
$29.99 USA/£28.99 UK
$39.99 CAN

Master Office 97 VISUALLY

ISBN 0-7645-6036-0
$39.99 USA/£36.99 UK
$54.99 CAN

ALSO AVAILABLE!
Master Microsoft® Office 2000 VISUALLY

ISBN 0-7645-6050-6
$39.99 USA/£36.99 UK
$54.99 CAN

FOR CORPORATE ORDERS, PLEASE CALL: 1-800-469-6616